THE VICTORIAN FLIGHT.

RUSSELL CONWELL AND THE CRISIS OF AMERICAN INDIVIDUALISM

Daniel W. Bjork

University Press
of America™

ISBN: 0-8191-0464-7
Library of Congress # 78-50767

To my parents who made it possible
Victor D. and Grace L. Bjork

CONTENTS

PREFACE

Russell Herman Conwell lived a long time, 1843 to 1925. His life spanned the transition from an agrarian to an urban-industrial America. In life he delivered one of America's most popular lectures. "Acres of Diamonds" was heard thousands of times by several million native listeners. The lecture's success helped finance Temple University in Philadelphia. Conwell founded Temple as well as a related church and hospital during the 1880's and 1890's. His reputation grew from the popularity of "Acres of Diamonds" and from his creative endeavors in Philadelphia. To the public that knew him the kaleidoscope of other roles—a Civil War officer, writer, newspaper correspondent and editor, lawyer, preacher, administrator, and world traveler—were embellishments of, not determiners of fame. But whatever the dimensions of Conwell's popular reputation, he was not a giant figure in late nineteenth and early twentieth century America; he was no Andrew Carnegie or Theodore Roosevelt.

So why a book about Russell Conwell? Certainly the rationale is not that all secondary personalities deserve biographies. This book does not pretend to be a full account of Conwell's life. Its object is revealed in the faith that some lives have striking symbolic importance. Conwell is interpreted as a symbol of a broad cultural transition. His experiences, language, and institutional creations dramatize something kept out of sight in a most changeable era in the American past. He is illustrative, even allegorical. His life is emblematic of the exchange between rapidly changing American forms and inner experience. In this tension, as it materialized in Conwell, is a window into a crisis in American individualism. Hopefully a symbolic Russell Conwell will illuminate the psychological predicament of an America passing into modernity.

The list of those who contributed toward the completion of this project is small but essential. Mrs. Miriam Crawford, curator of the Templana Collection at Temple University in Philadelphia, gave much time, insight, and labor to the writer's sometimes fumbling attempts to pry into Conwell's past. Miss Amelia Walston of Birmingham, Alabama typed and proofed the manuscript with keen professional eyes. Professors Robert Shalhope and H. Wayne Morgan of the University of Oklahoma in Norman offered many insights the author preempted as his own. Their critical efforts at several stages of revision made each draft seem far superior to the last. I am deeply in the debt of Professor David Levy, also of the University of Oklahoma, who guided impetuous judgments to a maturity which was inconceivable without his wisdom. Levy's invaluable critique of a student's dissertation was only matched by his careful judgment which helped turn the affair into a book. My wife, Rhonda, deserves all the superlatives reserved for wives on these occasions with one amendment. Her sacrifices included making astute criticisms of both the content and style, even when she knew the wrath of an over-sensitive husband would be forthcoming. Of course, none of the above share a whit for the book's shortcomings. They are the writer's alone.

Daniel W. Bjork
University of Alabama in
Birmingham
Fall, 1974

vi

ILLUSTRATIONS
of
RUSSELL H. CONWELL

Plate

PLATE I

PLATE II

PLATE III

PLATE IV

PLATE V

1

A COSTLY REPUTATION

"Be your own self. Be on the outside what you are on the inside."

> —Russell H. Conwell, *The New Day or Fresh Opportunities, A Book for Young Men.* [1]

"He counted his days that they might accomplish the work of two, himself and Johnny Ring, who seemed ever to be in his thoughts. This was the secret of his tireless and continuous service; this was the mainspring of all his endeavors and objectives"

> —Arthur Emerson Harris, *Personal Glimpses of Russell H. Conwell.* [2]

Russell Conwell as an old man looked back to his childhood with limited recall. Although he often spoke of the importance of correct child-rearing and never tired of reconstructing the early years of other famous men, he was lax about the specifics of his own boyhood. [3] Martin Conwell, Russell's father, was a small farmer in the Massachusetts hamlet of South Worthington, set in the rugged stony hills of the Berkshire region in the western part of the state. Martin had moved from Baltimore into the area probably sometime during the 1830's. Russell remembered his father as a man "always in a hurry." [4] The rocky soil of the Berkshires was covered with profuse underbrush making farming at best difficult. To supplement the family income Martin labored as a stone mason and sold handicrafts in the nearby trading center of Springfield. The days were long and hard for a farmer in Western Massachusetts in the mid-nineteenth century, the rewards meager. Throughout the last half of the Victorian century New England farmers were in the throes of a regional agricultural depression.[5] Russell was sure that the hardships of making a living from the grudging soil sent Martin to his grave in 1874 at age sixty-two. His mother, whose maiden name was Miranda Wickham, was not as fortunate; she died in 1877, only sixty. Miranda, whose family emigrated from New York State, bore Martin four children of whom Russell was the second. An infant brother lived only seven months and was buried outside South Worthington in the Ringville Cemetery in the spring of 1855. His older brother, Charles, died of consumption in 1869 at twenty-nine. A younger sister, Harriet (Russell called her Hattie), lived only into middle age. Martin, Miranda, Charles, Harriet, and the infant Arthur still lie together in the family plot in Ringville Cemetery two miles from the Conwell farm. Only Russell was buried elsewhere; for although he was to return frequently to South Worthington, his life in many ways was an abandonment of his rural beginnings.[6]

It was not surprising Conwell remembered so little that was distinct or illuminating about his parents. The drudgery of farming coupled with a strict rural Methodist morality allowed for few experiences outside the daily chores. What he did recall were exceptions to the farming routine. Conwell was fond of mentioning that John Brown, Frederick Douglass, and William Cullen Bryant visited the farm. He remembered that the family homestead was a stop on the underground railroad. Through the railroad Martin Conwell became acquainted with John Brown. An elderly Russell Conwell recalled that Brown and Martin went into business selling an assortment of goods in Springfield. But given Brown's aptitude for business and Martin's time-consuming duties on the farm, their partnership was a short one.[7] If the Conwell farm was from time to time graced with visits from famous guests, the arrivals were infrequent and their duration short. That Russell repeatedly recalled these visits only testified to the monotonous existence which permeated rural life. For thousands of New England farmers the work was terribly hard and often discouraging; it numbed the mind and broke the body.

2

There was, despite the dullness and the hard work, a certain romance to living in the highlands of Western Massachusetts—especially if one was a young lad taken with day-dreaming instead of the tedium of farm chores. From atop the quickly wooded and steeply inclined hills a boy could see the neighboring communities of Ringville and Worthington. On particularly clear days he noticed smoke rising from a factory in Northhampton to the east or Westfield to the south, both some fifteen to twenty miles distant. On such days he perhaps yearned to catch a sign of Springfield thirty-odd miles on the eastern horizon. Occasionally he probably imagined spotting Boston far, far away through the misty hills. During those times when he fled the all-too-real exertions of the barnyard for the solitude and ease of the highlands his fancy must have soared worlds beyond the tops of the lovely hills which surrounded him.[8] Thousands of adventure-filled miles beyond Boston were the cities of Europe he had heard travelers discuss, places he read about in school and in the Springfield paper. And after Europe there was the mysterious Near East and beyond it the elusive Orient. Could South Worthington and the family farm compare with all this? With his parents giving every ounce of their strength toward liquidating the twelve-hundred-dollar mortgage on their farm, little hope remained that they would take him to Boston, let alone to those bedazzling places across the sea. It was enough to make a boy scheme.

Russell found little respite from the labors of the farm at the local school. The prevailing educational methodology held that the mind was simply a muscle needing only regular exercise to keep it healthy and strong. The grammar school in Ringville administered to the neighborhood children a large dose of rote learning. Russell mastered the technique well, and later was able to repeat from memory the first two books of Milton's "Paradise Lost," along with a good portion of Blackstone. Later he learned several languages by rote while traveling between his home in Somerville and his work in Boston. The youngster did not, however, like the rigors of the New England schoolhouse. Even as an old man and president of a large university Conwell never disguised contempt for what passed for education in his youth. He spoke of the Ringville school as, "a motley gathering of all ages and grades ... [whose] teachers were a strange conglomeration of Latin, Greek, mathematics, ancient history,

3

spelling, and whipping. . . ." He recalled that he "was whipped eight times in one day, and usually for laughing at something which the teacher did not think funny."[9] Russell's revolt against the drudgery and boredom of the farm was not his only rebellion. From age three when he and Charles trudged two miles to the Ringville school until age fourteen when he left for the Wilbraham Academy outside Springfield, schooling bored Russell. In a negative way it added to a youthful propensity to dream of a destiny far removed from the confines of farm and school.[10]

Russell took matters into his own hands. Dreaming of exotic places was not enough; he had to do something. At thirteen, Conwell deserted family and farm and went to Boston to seek his fortune. But Boston was just a stop on a much more ambitious journey. His object was to seek passage to the Near East where adventure was as common as labor on the farm. Years later he reminisced that the "smallness of our cottage—compared with the wonderful wealth and luxury of Babylon—filled me with discontent, and I chafed at our homely labors and rebelled at the fare found on our table." How suffocating his own existence seemed when, ". . . there were great worlds for me to conquer, which I could never find in my native hills." He remembered reading in the *New York Ledger* of a runaway boy who became a comrade of Captain Kidd. Conwell recalled how, "the adventures of this boy and the great boxes of gold which he found buried in the sand were a continual harassment to me."[11] In his mind this tale of travel and riches kindled the fire of release which was smouldering deep in his young psyche. Slopping hogs and cutting wood could not compete with Captain Kidd.

Conwell's first flight ended in Boston. The thirteen-year-old quickly spent his store of cash on train fare and wandered the city streets looking for odd jobs. Narrowly missing arrest when an Irish policeman charged him with vagrancy and dog-tired from his journey, Russell went to bed hungry in a discarded hogshead. The deacon of a local mission awakened the now ravenous traveler and kindly offered a free breakfast. His benefactor then purchased the young runaway a train ticket back to Worthington. There was no argument. The now disillusioned Conwell was only too glad to escape the terrors of a hostile city and return to the family farm. But within two years the roaming urge struck Russell again.

This time Conwell not only left home but also country. With parental permission he worked his way from New York City to Liverpool on a cattle steamer. He wandered Europe for several months before returning to South Worthington.[12] Few boys of fifteen in Massachusetts were world travelers. Russell Conwell no longer had to climb hills to dream of faraway places; he could tell anyone who asked about their mysteries. The youngster's fund of experience was beginning to surpass that of his parents and neighbors. To stay in South Worthington and help his struggling parents on the farm seemed more stultifying than ever. Here was a young man who not only saw Europe, but was also attending the Wilbraham Academy. At this methodist institution, the equivalent of a private high school, Russell did two things which embellished his rising reputation. First, he joined the Old Club Debating Society which drew attention to his developing powers of elocution. Second, after supporting himself with scattered work his first year, he was given a teaching appointment in speech and reading.[13] At sixteen he was teaching young men at a locally-known academy, establishing a reputation with oratory, and was a European traveler. These were no common accomplishments for a teenager who lived in rural New England in the 1850's.

His parents' feelings were probably mixed. Martin and Miranda Conwell were proud of Russell. He was bringing their humdrum lives notoriety. The queries of neighbors about the up-and-coming youngster fed their pride. Yet the pain of having one of their own leave the farm for the attractions of the city and Europe hurt. Like most New England farmers, they wanted to give their sons a quality education, but for a purpose. If the boy decided he did not wish to farm then at least he could obtain a profession and come back to the hamlet to apply his new skill. Russell was different. He had set a pattern of wandering and it was doubtful if the environs of rural Massachusetts would satisfy his ambitions.[14]

Even though the desertion of young men for the lure of the city had been a common American scenario since the seventeenth century, the personal effect on parents was often devastating. To have worked a lifetime on the land and have sons refuse the legacy produced parental anxiety and resentment. With the prospects of war between the North and

South increasing daily the Conwells knew that Charles would enlist. How long would Russell stay behind to help on the farm? If one son were killed in the war and the other afflicted with wander-lust, what would happen to the farm when they were too old to work it? When Lincoln assumed the Presidency and the Southern states began to secede these were not hypothetical questions for the Conwells. At such times well-meaning parents might ask whether all the toil and trouble for their children was worth the effort. Although these anxieties clouded the future, Martin and Miranda could not deny Russell's request to go to college. After all, he was working his way toward an importance they could share.

Yale College, in Russell's mind, was an institution of higher learning that appreciated the aspirations of the struggling working boy. Fresh from working his way through Wilbraham, Russell knew he could expect only a pittance from home. But with Yale's bias for poor boys and the energies of an aspiring youth Conwell did not hesitate. Late in 1860 he enrolled with a special interest in law. His ebullient expectations were quickly dashed. Life at New Haven was markedly different from Wilbraham.In contrast to the egalitarian atmosphere there, Russell found Yale pervaded with social snobbery. No one knew or cared about his recent accomplishments. Many of the students knew Europe, more than a few were skilled debaters, and the campus seemed filled with student teachers and tutors. Life away from South Worthington, once apparently filled with wondrous adventure, now only induced inferiority feelings. Everybody seemed to have money except him. Social inadequacy accentuated his indigence. Russell dwelt on the gulf between their affluence and his personal poverty; he brooded over their aristocratic airs and his country bumptiousness. He kept to himself and began to read books on agnosticism. His aggressive self-assertiveness turned inward and began to change into a radical atheism.[15] But the attack on Fort Sumter moved Russell Conwell's mind and personality toward another opportunity.

When the Civil War started in the spring of 1861 Conwell was barely eighteen years old. He attempted to enlist immediately but Martin Conwell objected. One son in the army was enough; Russell went back to Yale. Other forces, however, thwarted his father's will. The tide of initial public enthusiasm and the young man's continual nagging changed the elder Conwell's mind. In 1862, at nineteen, Russell was allowed to enter the military. The enthralled youth rushed back to South Worthington. There he quickly added another accomplishment to his local reputation. Lincoln and the Massachusetts governor, John Andrew, were calling for volunteers; men were needed to seek out recruits. Conwell had all the ingredients to be a successful recruiter in Western Massachusetts. He had a strong voice, was aggressive, and was known. Word of his talents reached Governor Andrew and Conwell received a commission as captain in the forty-sixth Massachusetts Volunteer Militia. A letter written to Jenny Hayden, later to be Russell's first wife, from Jenny's father reveals something of the young man's oratory. Not only men attended the recruiting speeches:

> ... the ladies were all in love with him, a man told me so who was witness, said that when R. H. C. [Conwell] took the stand they showered Bokays [sic] all around him, when he to all appearances seemed quite overcome and wilted like a cabbage leaf in the July sun.[16]

To have responded so humbly to the adulation of local ladies did not diminish his popularity. It proved his Victorian sensibilities were impeccable.

As a recruiter Russell became fully aware of the power of his voice and the electrifying impact it had on audiences. From early childhood he had taken an interest in elocution. His mother claimed that at age six he regularly gave sermons to barnyard animals.[17] According to one listener his voice had a cultured quality that was almost ethereal:

> The young man is weirdly like his native hills. You can hear the cascades and the trickling streams in his tone of voice. He has a strange and unconscious power of so modulating his voice as to suggest the howl of the tempest in rocky declivities, or the soft echo of music in distant valleys. There would be great difference of opinion about his cleverness as a debater, but the breezy freshness and natural suggestiveness of varied nature in its wild state was completely fascinating. He excelled in description, and the auditor could almost hear the Niagara roll as he described it, and listened to catch the sounds of sighing pines. ... He was so unlike any other speaker, so completely natural that his blunders disarmed criticism.[18]

When such a voice captivated an audience at the height of an era of idealism it was little wonder Russell became a local legend before his twentieth birthday. There was more. The accolades gave him a taste of personal fame. He began to feel that people needed him. His voice was becoming the bridge between what the public wanted to hear and the notoriety he sought. But nothing was distinct yet. War-fever raced through him and captured his emotions as his voice shaped his fame. The great national excitement of the early 1860's did little to calm the expectations of a youth beginning to feel extraordinary powers.

The Civil War was the most dramatic and possibly the most significant experience Americans had in the nineteenth century. For Southerners the war was a defense of a special way of life. An alien society from the North was trying to shatter beloved social institutions which had been carefully wrapped in a protective ideology. For Northerners and young New Englanders, like Russell Conwell, the South was preventing the spread of free institutions and threatening the life of the Union. Conwell's duty was clear; he must protect his own. It went beyond that. There were deeply felt Americanisms to save. The flag, a birthright, a heritage, and the future were at stake. The threat to these symbols, both North and South, made countless soldiers the victims of whirling minds and emotions. Likely young Conwell's heart was in his throat as he made his way to training camp in Springfield in the autumn of 1862. The early phase of the war had not gone well. Bull Run was something to forget and McClellan's caution on the Virginia front was not reassuring. Surely F Company, as his outfit was called, would do honor for the forty-sixth Massachusetts Volunteer Militia. But Captain Conwell was to be disappointed. In November F Company went south to Newberne, North Carolina for a month of drilling and digging trenches. When they finally got close to the fighting their job "was to carry off the wounded and bury the dead."[19]

With no fighting Conwell had plenty of time to think about war and about himself. He had left Massachusetts as a minor celebrity and certainly did not expect military service to diminish his fame. Besides, people were beginning to expect great things from him, as he was of himself. What would he write home? Digging trenches and burying the dead were not objects of great interest in South Worthington. To make matters

8

more demanding he was engaged to Jenny Hayden who must be expecting news of a more heroic quality. Russell was equal to the occasion. A letter of December 24, 1862 was full of descriptions of mutilated bodies: "there on the bank of the River with one leg shot off, and all covered with tar and turpentine which burned and fried out his flesh, lay the unfortunate Rebel writhing in terrible agony."[20] A rather impressive Christmas Eve message for a young man to send his bride-to-be! Seven years later Conwell would roam the South as a professional observer for the Boston *Traveler* writing a feature on battlefields of the Civil War.[21] At the time, however, he was hardly thinking of a future career as a writer; the meaning of the War was too immediate and overwhelming for such reflection.

In 1863 the young soldier's term of service expired, and he quickly reenlisted. Governor Andrew asked Conwell to do more recruiting in the Berkshires. His ability to draw men to a cause was recognized and would be utilized time and time again. Still, something was missing: the enormous psychological impact of the War made him feel unfulfilled without direct participation. His second enlistment appeared to be a repetition of the first as he was again stationed at Newberne, North Carolina. Immediately thereafter the Second Massachusetts Regiment moved a short distance to Newport. While out on patrol he was hit, but saved when his watch blunted the shell's impact. A second time, while searching for horse feed he received what was thought at the time a minor shoulder wound.[22] These close calls did not diminish Conwell's thirst for the excitement of war. Patrol duty lacked the histrionics of a full-fledged battle. Anything less was not in keeping with the moral imperatives of war, to say nothing of the demands of a growing reputation. Something dramatic had to happen.

The uneventful days dragged on. The job of the Second Massachusetts Regiment was to protect supply depots along the Atlantic coast. This meant that Captain Conwell went on frequent short forages to insure his company had the appropriate stores to protect the fort at Newport. On one such trip he stopped at a farmhouse for a cooling draft of persimmon beer. He became ill and was delayed in returning to Newport. Upon arrival Conwell found the company uneasy because they had not received back pay. To retain the men's good will he made an unauthorized trip to Newberne to collect their salaries. Then the unexpected happened. With their commanding officer absent a Confederate raiding party surprised Conwell's men. Disgruntled over their pay claim and lacking leadership they abandoned the fort to the enemy. When he arrived in Newberne, Conwell learned the fate of his post. Sickened and panicky but knowing his duty he tried unsuccessfully to reach Newport. The denouement of an uneventful military career seemed imminent. How would he explain his unapproved absence to the authorities? What would Jenny think of her brave fiance? How could he ever return to parents and friends in South Worthington except on a rail? The rising star of Russell Conwell seemed eclipsed.

But the war produced paradoxes. What on the surface looked like a mortal blow to an ambitious idealistic young man became transformed into one of his "finest hours." During Conwell's second command he developed a friendship with a young boy of sixteen or seventeen, Johnny Ring. Ring came from Western Massachusetts and probably knew Russell before the War.[23] For Ring the relationship verged on idolatry. He spent hours polishing a sword that was presented to Captain Conwell during the latter's first command. Although Johnny regretted that Russell did not believe in the Bible, it was clear the boy felt he was near one of the noblest of men. When Conwell learned of the disaster at Newport he was also told of Johnny Ring's tragic death. Johnny was killed trying to return to Captain Conwell while crossing a burning bridge. His dying words were supposedly, "Tell the Captain I saved his sword."[24]

Here was an infusion of idealism to counter the shame of being accused of abandoning his command. If one of his men sacrificed his life to return a sword to the commanding officer was not Conwell's loyalty vindicated? He did have the best interests of his men in mind. He tried to retrieve their pay. They agreed that he had attempted to return to them. But army officials saw it differently. Russell Conwell was dishonorably discharged. His court-martial asserted that "Captain R. H. Conwell, 2d Massachusetts artillery, did, in the face of the enemy, shamefully abandon his command...."[25] He returned to Massachusetts claiming his innocence, but humbly accepting the court's verdict. Conwell's friends, however, would not take this injustice without a fight. As Johnny Ring's body returned to the Ringville cemetery, word of his devoted loyalty to Conwell traveled fast. Comrades from the Massachusetts Second tried without success to have him reinstated as their commander. Russell was urged to go to Washington and see Lincoln; he saw the President but the decision stood. In the meantime a friend wrote General James McPherson recommending the court-martialed captain as a staff officer. McPherson granted Conwell an interview at his command in Chattanooga, Tennessee and appointed him lieutenant-colonel. The details of the court-martial were unclear to the General and the young man had fine credentials. By 1864 Conwell may have been in active duty again, in the vicinity of Kenesaw Mountain, Georgia.

Russell's dishonorable discharge, despite the Johnny Ring deliverance, shook the twenty-one year old soldier. His friends had vindicated his innocense but doubts remained. For some reason the army that was spending its blood to save the Union had formally accused him of cowardice. Had he tried hard enough to get back to his men? Johnny Ring had objected to his religious scepticism and then died trying to find his Godless commanding officer. Outwardly he convinced those who knew and loved him of his valor, but inwardly was he certain? He needed to be sure of himself or the past might haunt him and the future be in doubt. The Battle of Kenesaw Mountain worked to remove these qualms and more; Russell *claimed* he was wounded severely and *left* for dead on the field.[26]

Lying among the dead and the dying, Conwell recalled pondering "the great riddle of life and death — the meaning and the purpose of it all...."[27] He remembered facing death to prove inner integrity, yet something was missing. Surely there was a way to transform a conviction into a commitment. Every trace of self-doubt, conscious or unconscious, must now be exorcised. It was not simply anxiety over his discharge and the Ring affair which needed expurging. There was the older matter of his steady abandonment of cultural roots which began with his hill-top dreams of Boston, Europe, and Babylon. Conwell's moral culpability, ironically, grew with his rise in reputation. He could not achieve the latter without the former.[28]

Every attempt to jettison the South Worthington heritage had left a moral debt. Fleeing physically to Boston and to Europe was part of it; so was the replacement of his parents' Methodism with atheism at Yale. He was not only different from his parents; he was leaving their place and their religion. Russell Conwell was creating an identity by saying the life of his parents was unacceptable. For a time the excitement of the War obscured the unfolding of this drama. The dishonorable discharge and Johnny Ring opened it up again on a new level of intensity. As long as Conwell achieved honor as a soldier he could neutralize the struggle between the older rural values and the need for fame; his parents partook of the same Northern ideology as he did. If the Civil War tore families and regions apart it brought as many together. For a brief period domestic and cultural struggles were subdued in the idealism of the emergency. But in Russell's mind the near destruction of his military career probably reopened the issue. Self-doubt reached more deeply than when at Yale. While in school he could convert to atheism without being fully aware of a mounting moral debt. Johnny Ring's attempt to return Conwell's sword was the catalyst which brought his guilt into consciousness. This young lad, imbued with the cultural heritage Russell was trying to abandon, died attempting to lead Conwell back to the Bible. Though in life Ring's pleas failed to reconnect his commander with religion, in death they did. More significantly Conwell's religious awakening was part of a larger reunion. He now embarked upon a reconstitution of parental values; the conversion was a return to cultural origins.

Russell Conwell was moved to religious conviction not because of any philosophical consideration of the "great riddle of life and death" but because for the first time he became fully aware of his doubt and guilt. The Johnny Ring episode became a primary symbol of young Conwell's central psychic struggle. It remained germane all his life. The Johnny Ring tale and the "Story of the Sword" were endlessly repeated.[29] To a man who built the first edifice of fame by running away from home and sharpened the estrangement with religious apostasy, the Ring lore was personally compelling.

When the Civil War ended an intellectual revolution came to the minds of many Northerners. The transcendental idealism of those who felt they could perfect man if he were freed from corrupt institutions seemed naive. Four painful years of war convinced large numbers of educated New Englanders that the romantic reformers of the ante-bellum period had pursued an anti-institutionalism to fanaticism. Their extreme perfectionism and individualism served only to defeat the forces of compromise and reason, hence bringing on the war. During the ordeal Northerners learned to look beyond personal agony to the more abstract goal of saving the Union. Individuals were expendable, the nation was not. Impersonal bureaucratic procedures were initiated in field hospitals to prevent good Samaritans from personally sympathizing with the sick. Military discipline was to be followed whatever the individual cost. The efficient, scientific organizationally-minded expert was the true patriot; sentimental talk of giving one's heart to the suffering was old-fashioned and worse, harmful to the Union's cause. Before the War the moral individual jettisoned evil institutions thus perfecting society; after the War society was protected with efficient institutions which ignored tender-hearted individuals. The operating assumptions of American individualism were being reversed. Many minds were bewildered. They had entered the fray to defend the free individual and the symbols which embodied him; at the War's end they seemed to defend the symbols of order and institutions at the individual's expense. A change of the first order was at hand.[30]

For Northerners, the ideology which fueled the War and the one which began to replace it was a compression of a principal tension in American life, one existing in acute form throughout the nineteenth and into the twentieth century. That tension encompassed Russell Conwell's life. Whether the story of change was told as the transformation of an agrarian into an industrial nation, as the move from individuality to institution-alization, or the abandonment of religious faith for scientific certainty, Conwell lived in these modulations. His psychic crisis was immeshed in this milieu.[31] If Russell assuaged the guilt which resulted from deserting his beginnings through religious dedication problems remained. These difficulties, like his guilt, were intimately set in the crunch of national change throughout the rest of the old and into the new century.

Conwell went back to South Worthington. Their son's new found religious faith made his aging parents thankful. There was another reason for their joy. Russell and Jenny Hayden had decided to marry immediately.[32] The young couple lived a few months in Springfield so Russell could get some experience in a law office. Then it was on to law school in Albany, late in 1865, where he could take advantage of his pre-law training at Yale and his reading of Blackstone in the army. Of course Martin and Miranda were disappointed that the young couple did not stay in South Worthington, but Springfield and Albany were within fifty miles. Their delight was short lived; again Conwell decided to leave home. This time he would go west, not to farm, but to practice law in the bustling twin cities of Minneapolis and St. Paul. His ambition and the direction of America's growth made the choice seem natural. Development was rapid in the urban Northwest. Cities like Chicago, Milwaukee, Minneapolis-St. Paul, and Des Moines were booming. A young lawyer could build a solid practice here faster than in the East, and could work for Christ's cause as well in Minnesota as in Massachusetts. After the veneer of his war experience and the pride in going to law school wore off, the old surroundings appeared dull. His parents had aged rapidly and the monotony of childhood friends and haunts were too much to bear. It was a fitting time to move.

But these practical reasons to migrate were the window-dressing of a more fundamental situation. Russell's life was already entwined in a surprising number of roles: son, farm-boy, runaway, student, European traveler, debater, teacher, atheist, recruiter, soldier, commander, deserter, hero, husband, and lawyer. The multiplicity of roles hinted at an identity crisis of no small magnitude. Most of Conwell's roles demanded that he move physically or socially from his beginnings. He found that he gained reputation as he acquired roles. Each new position and place put more distance between his childhood and young adulthood. As Conwell grew up he grew away. Not simply away from childhood, but away from the security of knowing who he was. While he lost identity he gained reputation; to continually shed identity was to acquire fame. This chameleon-like quality not only induced self-doubt, but produced a compulsion to continue changing colors. It was a drama played out often in nineteenth century America. As the nation traveled further and further from its beginnings American identity collapsed into a kaleidoscope of change. The more industrial, institutional, and urban it became the more strained the longing for its fading identity—the rural past. In such a society roles multiplied with bewildering speed and the need to extol the genuine individual, an arch-type American who knew himself and his values,

14

increased. Yet the reputation of the nation required inflating the tempo of change. To gain wealth and power America forsook its early heritage of farms, stable callings, and churches. Identity crumbled as national adulthood was being achieved.[33] So it was with Conwell. In the act of becoming a man, of achieving a more satisfying life, he amputated a rural past that returned to perplex him. The process would not be reversed for either Conwell or the nation. Cultural roots were too deep to be forgotten, and the impetus toward fame and fortune too strong to resist.

For seventeen years, from 1865 to 1882, Conwell continued amassing a reputation before it ossified into fame. He stayed in Minnesota only three years, but managed to edit a newspaper, organize a Young Men's Christian Association, practice law, sell real estate, and recruit for the local Grand Army of the Republic.[34] When he left Minneapolis because of failing health in 1868, he obtained an appointment as immigration agent to Germany. He left Jenny in Massachusetts while he traveled in Europe to regain vigor.[35] In 1869 he returned and secured a position as traveling correspondent for the Boston *Traveler* and later with the New York *Tribune*. Although throughout the seventies and into the 1880's Conwell lived in Massachusetts he was gone much of the time. The duties of a correspondent and public lecturer for the Redpath lecture agency kept him journeying through the states, Europe, and even the Orient.[36] During the 1870's he practiced law in Boston and promoted real estate in the growing suburb of Somerville. As in Minneapolis, Conwell got involved in organizing young men. This time he applied his organization expertise for Boston's Tremont Temple and recruited a huge Bible class which peaked at two thousand.[37] The full schedule did not deter him from writing a number of books, including several campaign biographies for the Republican party.[38]

On one level, this frenzy of activity rewarded Conwell, and by the beginning of the eighties he was verging on a national reputation. His blue chip lecture "Acres of Diamonds" was beginning to gain wide notoriety.[39] Bostonians and others in the Northeast had read in the *Traveler* "Russell's Letters from the Battlefields." Others had sampled the patriotic biographies of Grant, Hayes, Garfield, and Blaine. In Boston he built a reputation defending unpopular cases for small fees and was

15

known as a "people's lawyer." As His experiences and roles increased so did the fame.[40]

On another level he was again made aware of how he was emasculating the past. The first blow was the death of his wife in 1872.[41] She bore him two children, Nima and Leon, and was his faithful companion for seven years. But had he returned her love and care? Conwell traveled much of the time. It was not easy to move to strange surroundings in the late nineteenth century. She had agreed to go to Minnesota but the move could not have helped her health. Perhaps Jenny would still be alive if he had been more sensitive to her than to his career.[42] Is it not reasonable to suppose that an ambitious young man who lost a beloved wife would blame himself? He must have had second thoughts. If he had only stayed nearer home, closer to both their beginnings. Perhaps looking at his motherless children reminded him of a familiar anxiety: maybe she had died to remind him he had deserted her. The Civil War self-reproach could have been reenacted. Conwell rededicated his life to Christ and began studying the Bible intensely.[43]

In 1874 Martin Conwell died. Miranda was left with the farm as her daughter Harriet had married and her first born, Charles, had died in 1869. Russell did not move back to South Worthington, but did move closer toward the ministry. He met and became engaged to Sarah Sanborn, of Newton Center, Massachusetts. Miss Sanborn lived near the Newton Theological Seminary and grew up in a wealthy family. She also took a lively interest in evangelical religion. Here was a woman who could be both a mother to Nima and Leon and a Christian comfort to a bereaved and even guilty Conwell. The disintegration of Conwell's family with the deaths of his wife and father had direct bearing on essential psychological balance. Without remarrying and seeking the ministry he would carry the burden of abandonment. The time had come to make his Christian commitment more than a predilection; he would enter the ministry after his marriage. Late in 1874 Sarah and Russell were wed.[44]

For a time Conwell practiced law in Boston, but entered Newton Theological Seminary on a part-time basis. Sometime in the late seventies he became involved in the financial reconstruction of a near defunct small Baptist church in Lexington several miles outside Boston. A parishioner of the church, interestingly a young widow, engaged Conwell to liquidate or renovate the property which was all but abandoned. Here was a challenge to restore the past, an opportunity to reconstitute rather than desert. Here was the chance to turn his talents toward reconstruction without moving from Massachusetts. He announced he would address the dwindling congregation. Word traveled fast. When it was learned the noted lecturer and author, Russell Conwell, was engaged to save their church and would make an address the building overflowed with the curious.[45] After a successful debut he organized a subscription campaign to build a new structure. To raise the initial capital, a community fair worked beyond expectations. Conwell then reorganized the internal structure and operations of the church from Sunday School to the music program, and the new organization thrived. Word spread beyond Massachusetts of the organizational genius of the young lawyer-preacher. Somehow being ordained in 1879 was anti-climactic.[46]

When Conwell gave up a lucrative law practice in Boston for a small pulpit in Lexington some of his relatives thought he was demented.[47] Perhaps the strain of losing a wife and his parents within five years caused the young man to lose touch with the real world. Conwell's critics were right in thinking their deaths profoundly affected his decision. But it was the attempt to maintain his connection with their world that drove him into the ministry. How could he erase the sense of estrangement from his beginnings? A growing reputation did not repudiate guilt. Strangely, the more renowned Conwell became the more sensitive his need to clutch at abandoned and ever more fleeting origins. There was one sure way of preserving his equilibrium. He must turn his talent, energy, and reputation against his anxiety. The way to liquidate the psychological debt was to redirect personal assets toward receding cultural roots. Johnny Ring had pointed the way. For fifteen years, Conwell had groped for the right medium; at Lexington he found it. He would rebuild more than a church.

Conwell continued to lecture with Redpath and write books. "Acres of Diamonds" was now one of the best-known lectures in the country.[48] The small church prospered but the early excitement of using talent and notoriety for a Christian cause began to wear thin. The old dream of newer, and challenging worlds returned. Lexington, Massachusetts was simply too small and static for Conwell's energy, ability, and growing reputation. He waited for a fitting opportunity which came in 1882.

Several hundred miles south of Conwell's modest church in the village of Lexington lay the sprawling metropolis of Philadelphia, with over one million people in the early 1880's. Although New York was now the first city in the land, the City of Brotherly Love was still growing rapidly.[49] The section of town known as north Philadelphia was a burgeoning urban frontier. From downtown Philadelphia to the Reading railroad, which traversed the city east to west five or six miles to the north, stretched scrattered urban development mixed with rural land. Broad Street, the major north-south thoroughfare, was only partially surfaced and horse-car service extended only a fraction of the length. North Philadelphia was booming; it was not very different from the Minneapolis Russell and Jenny moved to in the late sixties.[50]

The Grace Baptist Church was formed in 1872 to serve the religious need in the expanding north Philadelphia section. Grace Church was situated on Broad between Montgomery and Berks streets about two miles south of the Reading railroad. Early services were held in a tent, but numbers soon made this arrangement impossible. In 1875 construction was begun on a larger and more permanent structure. Financial difficulties became acute during the depression of the 1870's and the church mortgage was temporarily foreclosed. Seven years later the building was still not completed and the mortgage remained a substantial fifteen thousand dollars. The church deacons were uncomfortable; something or someone had to complete the church and liquidate the mortgage.[51] A member of the congregation told the Grace Church deacons of an amazing young minister from Massachusetts, Russell Conwell. Perhaps some of the church leaders had heard "Acres of Diamonds" and remembered the name. The parishioner went on to tell of Conwell's resurrection of the near dead Lexington church. Here was a man who knew how to get things done—without saddling a church with an enormous debt. But an offer must be made quickly, and the deacons acted. They contacted Conwell and invited him to Philadelphia to consider the Grace Church.

He was impressed. The Philadelphians offered an annual salary of three thousand dollars, a parsonage, and the

18

opportunity to fulfill outstanding engagements with the Redpath Lyceum.[52] Conwell was approaching forty, not old, but no longer young. Jenny had been gone ten years and his parents were now memories. Nima and Leon were almost teenagers and Sarah had given him another daughter, Agnes, who was already in school.[53] It would be advantageous to have a higher salary, but that was secondary in view of Sarah's wealth. The main consideration was time. If he were to fully apply his energies he must do it now, before the inertia of approaching old age. Philadelphia was a city large enough for his reputation. He could only embellish it here. They needed him. The Conwells arrived at the parsonage on Broad Street to stay on Thanksgiving night 1882. The story of a unique institutional development was about to unfold. Conwell's internal struggle moved to another plane of resolution.

When Russell Conwell settled into the new pastorate in Philadelphia he did not find repose. Philadelphia was part of a national vortex of change. The industrial revolution gathered strength throughout the nineteenth century, but climaxed between the Civil War and World War I. The industrial convulsion accomplished no less than a massive exchange of local, agrarian, petty capitalistic communities for cosmopolitan, urban, corporate industrial systems. A relatively structureless, highly personalized, and inward-looking mode of life was being forged into an anonymous, encircling society. America was opening itself to the wholesale and complex unity of modernity; it was breaking down the introspection and simplistic communitarianism of its rural past. The overwhelming presence of growth, production, and organization, generating into new institutional forms, was part of the transformation. So was the breakdown of traditional communities, the multiplicity and confusion of roles, and nostalgia for the fading rural past. One set of developments appeared the obverse of others. Antipodes reigned and Conwell's Philadelphia did not escape the contradictions accompanying national change.[54]

The quintessence of American transformation in the eighties and nineties was not the annihilation of the nation's rural past. Modernity did not destroy but merely displaced the older agrarian tradition. Conwell's activity in Philadelphia was symbolic of both the modernization and the displacement. The story of the growth of Conwellian institutions reenacted the central strains in a larger, national drama. It offered a view of the past and present colliding, in a man whose personality embodied the contradictions of a Victorian America which was losing its cultural grip.

At first it appeared that Conwell's resurrection of the mortgage-laden Grace Baptist Church was a grander repetition of the Lexington renascence. Within a few months the church was constructed and the mortgage retired.[55] As word traveled of the new preacher's superb oratory the curious besieged the new church. Grace Church was built to accommodate several hundred but before long crowds triple that size were packing the structure and overflowing into Broad Street. Something had to be done. Conwell began issuing free admission tickets. This temporarily helped control the throngs, but created local criticism. Some spoke scoffingly of "Conwell's church." Others spread the rumor that an avaricious pastor charged money for admission to the Grace Church. Somehow adequate room had to be provided, without tickets.[56]

The obvious answer was a larger church, but the congregation had just finished paying for a new church, and the deacons would not readily agree to new indebtedness. Then, too, some critics characterized Conwell's ministry as charlatanry. Would not the construction of a larger church provide fuel to those who spoke already of "Conwell's folly"?[57] Yet he was already popular and church membership was never higher. He had come to Philadelphia with the reputation of an innovator. People would expect a dramatic move. Still he needed a pretext to act; something which would unify the congregation behind financing a new church. If the parishioners were on his side the deacons would surely accept the project.

Whether consciously or unconsciously, the major inner tension in Conwell's life came into play when he decided to build a larger church. The old theme of abandonment and reconnection returned in a different form. His desire to rally the congregation for the new church was a symbolic excursion into his most compelling need. The pretext was the death of a little girl, Hattie Wiatt. One Sunday in 1884 Conwell came upon a tearful six-year-old child who, because of over-crowding, was denied admittance to Sunday School. The broad-shouldered pastor, moved by Hattie's plight, lifted the small girl to his back and carried her to the school. Conwell comforted her, explained

20

the over-crowding and the need for larger facilities, and then forgot the incident. The child immediately resolved to save her money so a spacious church might be built. Her idea became known several weeks later when she suddenly contracted diphtheria and died; Hattie had saved fifty-seven cents for a larger church.[58] Here was an experience which struck a familiar chord in Conwell's psyche, one which could be molded to the deepest needs of his personality. Hattie was trying to seek spiritual guidance and the church had ignored her plea; it forsook a child's need for Christian direction. But she, like Johnny Ring, had tried to point to the Christian solution. Her death and the revelation of saved pennies carried the same meaning as Johnny Ring's self-sacrifice for his hero's sword. Conwell had not heeded Johnny's admonition to accept the Bible; neither had he immediately caught the full-force of Hattie's desire to go to Sunday School. These episodes were rooted in guilt and revealed Conwell's determination to prove his worth and expiate that guilt. And they pointed to a related problem. Both cases reminded Conwell of the way he had lost identity and gained reputation; he had repeatedly abandoned loved ones and surroundings for advancement. In the Ring case he absolved culpability through conversion. After Jenny's death and the demise of his father Conwell entered the ministry. By now the message was clear: only a reconnection with Christ could really erase the guilt. Christ was the contrasting metaphor of what one side of his life had been—ambition, the desire for power, and the grasp for reputation. Jesus was love, passivity, charity, and faith in the Father. Christ was a powerful symbol for what he felt the forsaken past must be. Hattie Wiatt evoked this old pattern. He would return and reunite with his early heritage once more.[59]

A problem remained for Conwell. As a young man he released tension when his anxieties were consumed in a battle-field conversion, and later through exchanging law for the pulpit. Philadelphia was different. The new industrial-urban milieu and the growing demands of fame made a simple conversion experience and a change of profession less satisfying. Spiritual transformation made sense on the battlefield for a young man who had abandoned his old religion. In Philadelphia a middle-aged pastor who claimed privileged communion with the Almighty might be branded a quack. This was an age when most Protestant ministers were trying to come to terms with Darwinian science. An open religious reawakening would be too risky to a man well aware of being on the verge of fame. He was a newcomer in a city of a million people, people who were seeking practical answers to confusions, disappointments, and tragedies of urban existence. A Dwight Moody might temporarily ignite the older Jacksonian revivalistic temper, but only for a moment. Moody moved on but Conwell was in Philadelphia to stay. There was a more fitting way to vindicate Hattie Wiatt and release the old anxiety.[60]

In the sunset of the nineteenth century large reputations were being forged. Renown was coming to men who created huge organizations which metamorphosed into permanent institutions. The names Rockefeller, Vanderbilt, Carnegie, Armour, and others were on many lips. Philadelphia's own John Wanamaker, while perhaps not in their league, had nonetheless become famous for developing America's first modern department store.[61] Conwell too had often shown organizational accomplishment. From the time he recruited soldiers in the Berkshires, to youth-oriented activities in Minneapolis and Boston, to the erection of a renovated Lexington church he excelled in manipulation for good causes. The time was ripe to use this talent in Philadelphia. He would build one of the largest churches in America. The meaning of Hattie Wiatt's death would not pass unattended. The connection between the child's wish and Conwell's inner struggle would be symbolically secured through the creation of a Christian institution. The new church would personify in stone, iron, stained glass, and good works the past he had left. It would stand as a permanent antithesis to all the broken connections and ambitious wanderings of his young manhood. The continuing Conwellian drama of leaving and returning was resolved on a new plane; one which displaced personal tensions into the making of a lasting institution. Conwell's shift from expending inner energies on conversion and the appropriation of a multitude of social roles was significant. The change was illustrative of a massive transformation in American life. The late nineteenth century saw the exchange of an open, individualistic, fluid society for a closing institutionalized and bureaucratic one. The change was never complete but was happening. Conwell's shift from a free-wheeling transient organizer into an occupationally sedentary institution-maker was consistent with the larger cultural phenomenon. His inner struggle and the differing modes of resolution were one man's psychic expression to an era of American redefinition. The personal and historical dynamics were intertwined: they each told something important about the other.

The new pastor saw financial potential in the Hattie Wiatt story. He promptly organized the church's young people between ages twelve and sixteen into a subscription organization. The Wiatt-Mite Society continued the collection of Hattie's pennies, and adult contributions followed. Money-raising campaigns such as fairs were instituted, and one large gift of ten thousand dollars combined to partially finance the dead girl's dream.[62] In September, 1886 a lot was purchased at Broad and Berks Streets within several blocks of the Grace Baptist Temple in 1886. When completed in March, 1891 the Temple accommodated over three thousand parishioners, making it the largest Protestant church in America.[63]

The architecture of the Temple showed graphically how a modern institution could displace the past. Its size and facilities were typical gadgets. Besides seating thousands of church-goers, the new temple had modern office facilities for the church staff. The offices were "equipped with desks, filing cabinets, telephones, speaking tubes and everything necessary to conduct the business of the church in a businesslike way."[64] The chairs in the sanctuary were cushioned and connected in curving rows making the interior like the latest amphitheater—it was a modern church.

Yet it was called the "Temple." The name had an ancient cast and so did the physical appearance of the building. The exterior of hewn stone gave the building a massive fortress-like appearance.[65] It was an impressive structure facing Broad Street, almost a castle, and produced a feeling of age. The Temple was modern but, from the exterior, historically remote. Inside the impression of modernity was also muted:

> The moment one enters the vast auditorium with its crimson chairs, its cheery carpet, its softly-tinted walls, one feels at home. Light filters in through rich windows, in memory of some member gone before, or of some class or organization. Behind the pulpit stands the organ, its rich-looking pipes rising almost to the roof. Everywhere is rich subdued coloring—not ostentatious, but cheery and homelike.[66]

23

The motif was one of gentle grandeur. A soft repose pervaded the place. In these confines a parishioner could lose the noise and irritations of the city. One could sink into a cushioned chair, listen to the soothing strains of the pipe-organ, and gaze at a pastoral scene in the stained-glass windows. It was not hard to be transported to another time.[67] The mind wandered back decades to childhood days when life seemed simpler, less strident, and more peaceful. Perhaps the past was alive for a few moments. Then the service ended and the real world impinged upon reverie. Conwell's church was a modern building with a traditional purpose.

This institutional environment served as a perfect stage for Conwell. From the pulpit he commanded an orderly audience which the veneer of the Temple's interior appointments helped put in a nostalgic mood. For nearly thirty-five years his words resounded in an atmosphere steeped in the trappings of reminiscence. Every Sunday he stepped into a modern institution that reinstated, for a moment, the remembered past. It was his creation and the very architecture captured an important tension in himself and in the nation: energy expended in the construction of institutions could recreate the past. The refrain was familiar in Conwell's life. Time and time again he would act or create to assuage the dissonance. Since the strain was instigated with a departure from the past and eased returning to it, the process could be self-perpetuating. Conwell's first institution was the arena of this crisis, a safe setting within which to act out his predicament.

Once an institutional resolution of these strains was found, the less feasible the earlier devices of conversion and role change became. There was no need to move. The middle-aged preacher was a local success story. But he did not stop with creating the Grace Baptist Temple; the Temple marked the beginning of a more grandiose project.

Before ground was broken for the church another institution was given a Conwellian beginning. As in the Wiatt story, an inspirational tale became the justification for organizational expansion. Sometime during the mid-1880's a young printer, Charles M. Davies, came to the Reverend Conwell asking for instruction in Greek and Latin. Davies was sure he wanted to enter the ministry. Conwell agreed to instruct the ambitious young man for one hour three evenings a week. When he arrived for his first lesson Davies brought along six other aspiring students. Conwell explained to them the sacrifices of getting an education but they were not deterred. At the second meeting forty boys attended the pastor's lecture. Out of this modest beginning an evening school with volunteer teachers was established.[68]

It made good sense for Conwell to agree to tutor Davies. His work experiences at Wilbraham and Yale gave him a sympathy for poor boys struggling to go beyond their circumstances. Davies came with hat in hand; he was humble and willing to work hard at Greek and Latin to become a minister. The Lord needed those with backbone. When the other young men showed up Conwell was pleasantly surprised. Here was a chance to explain the meaning not only of work, but loyalty, and devotion to Christian values. He would make sure these youngsters did not go astray and flirt with atheism as he had done. Conwell had often directed the activities of young men. His mind probably wandered back twenty-five years to the excitement of recruiting Union volunteers. The Y.M.C.A. activities in Minneapolis gave him a chance to guide the moral energies of youth, and the Bible class at Boston's Tremont Temple was a huge success. The more he thought about it, the more compelling the Christian organizing of young men became. The opportunity in Philadelphia was the best yet. A strong yearning likely emerged. He could not help but think of Johnny Ring. As Ring's commanding officer Conwell refused to take up the moral challenge of the boy that worshiped him. The old pain of abandonment could come back. Atonement worked before and now another chance to release the old self-doubt surfaced. Besides, there was a groundswell of congregational support for the new church.

The people were in the mood to organize behind the inspirational leadership of their new pastor. They expected dramatic moves. The Temple was being noticed and they wished to get involved, to be a part of all the excitement. The deacons, while not as enthusiastic as the congregation, agreed to support the new church. Why not take advantage of their receptivity? As the numbers hearing about Conwell's night school grew, the idea of creating a working man's college dominated his thoughts.

25

By the start of the second year of instruction over two hundred and fifty students were attending night classes. In 1887 Temple College was in regular operation. A year later the college was chartered with an enrollment of just under six hundred. The early college handbook outlined the policies the school would pursue. Tuition was free to all employed working people. Temple College was to provide for the higher educational needs of 30,000 "walking workers" who lived in the immediate area and 180,000 others who lived within a half-hour's horse-car ride. Other policies which Conwell endorsed included night class scheduling, the absence of sectarianism, the necessity of all students choosing a profession upon admission, and financial support through gifts, charity, and endowment. Temple was "to help ambitious working people become useful members of society and prestigious professionals." It was "to cultivate a taste for higher learning" so students would be encouraged to continue learning all their lives.[69] In 1891 the college granted degrees, and before 1900 was divided into separate schools—among others, liberal arts, law, and business. There was also a small program for physicians and a normal school for teachers. By the 1970's Temple University was educating approximately 40,000 full and part-time students.

Temple College grew steadily in the early 1890's. It was a time when a multitude of institutions of higher learning were being erected. In Chicago John D. Rockefeller was embellishing his spectacular career as endower of the University of Chicago.[70] Surely Conwell was aware of the accolades attending Massachusettsian George Peabody's earlier funding of the Peabody Institute in Nashville, Tennessee. Then, too, Anthony Drexel, the Philadelphia industrialist, had recently endowed Drexel Institute within several miles of Temple. These men were not merely wealthy, they were civic leaders. A close association with the public need for higher education enhanced their reputation. Beyond the public notoriety which came to major educational leaders there was the chance of building a major source of national progress. American higher education was the vanguard of technological advancement and the growth of professional expertise. Both were being planted in the urban world of the 1890's. The public was hopeful about colleges and universities because they promised social mobility for themselves and their children as well as expertise and power for the

26

nation. Surely Russell Conwell was well-aware of the rising importance of higher education.

The university represented America's direction. It was a place where young men and even women could achieve national and personal promise. If the west had less appeal as a frontier, an urban frontier was beckoning the young to fresh opportunities. The future was sought in school rather than in the soil; dreams were now realized within institutions not by crossing prairies. Since boyhood Conwell had been a visionary. Moving from one place to the next was one way of acting out his fancies. But as change closed in on him, escape over space was less viable as adventure. Traveling was still exciting, but not as central to his dreams. Ironically, Conwell now found adventure in a sense of place. He built an educational institution and retained the dream of advancement for both himself and society.[71] Conwell found the same release and self-satisfaction in helping others to achieve schooling as in abandoning his roots for new places. Slowly yet surely Conwell's energies were redirecting themselves. Certainly, he continued to lecture; "Acres of Diamonds" was more popular than ever. But now a preacher and an educator spoke to the throngs. While lecturing he sought out civic leaders in every city and town and requested donations for the new Temple College.[72] The future of the college and the character of young men depended on the generous audiences. They felt the change in national direction. What large town or small city did not have aspirations for a local college? Fifty years before such ambitions had seemed less urgent; now they mirrored the deepest needs of the republic. If America were to preserve her heritage of freedom and opportunity for all, higher education had to flourish. There was no better way to express this than by contributing to a college established to help working people advance. To do less was to endanger the nation's dream. In forty years Conwell marshaled over eight million dollars for Temple College and University.[73]

The college and church were different legal entities. Each was chartered separately. Yet their affairs were intertwined.[74] Only in 1911, when the college began to receive state funding, did the close monetary involvement end.[75] There was, however, never any doubt that Conwell was the inspirational and organizational driving force in founding both institutions.[76] He never, however, immersed himself in their day-to-day

27

operations. This was left, over the years, to a number of faithful lieutenants who saw that organizational procedures and policies were executed.[77] Conwell generated the kind of loyalty that perpetuated itself year after year through the force of his personality and social philosophy, but tried to steer clear of the every day bureaucracy of the Temple institutions.[78] The inexorable pull of organizations toward procedural pettiness never overcame him. He remained a seer with a message and a mission to the end of his days.[79] While the milieu in which Conwell created institutions changed immensely between the 1880's and the 1920's, Conwell's style did not, even though in its redirection toward institutional creation it found a new medium of expression.

It was always a matter of flight and return. If he saw the necessity of creating a church and a college to obliterate an old anxiety, Conwell also used those creations to escape the familiar. As the famous head of two up-and-coming urban establishments he retained a flamboyancy for action and innovation long after it was possible for him to implement his plans. The last Conwellian institutional creation came over thirty years before his death. It presaged more than the ubiquitous transformation from an innovational institutionalism to administrative bureaucracy. In establishing the Samaritan Hospital Conwell released inner anxiety a final time through creating a lasting institution.

Temple College was destined to become the largest organizational structure Conwell conceived, but the Samaritan Hospital was ultimately not far behind. The latter venture was begun late in 1891. Not surprisingly another inspirational story was associated with Conwell's part in its origin. The North Philadelphia Hospital, chartered in March of 1890 and located within walking distance from the Baptist Temple, closed its doors because of shaky finances. The need for a neighborhood hospital, however, remained. This region of Philadelphia was the scene of many industrially related accidents. Without a hospital many lives would needlessly be lost. A woman living in the neighborhood wrote Conwell of the necessity for a hospital in the area. Supposedly, he turned to a church secretary after reading the letter and responded, "Wherever there is a need I am wanted" and left immediately to inquire about the closed hospital.[80] Conwell found that the furniture and equipment in the hospital could be purchased, but a new building was needed to house the facility. He told the deacons of his plans to secure a property and reinstitute the neighborhood hospital. They were probably less than enthusiastic as the church was now heavily indebted both on its own account, and for helping finance the college. Conwell was not dissuaded. He discussed the matter with the congregation, pointing to the need for a local healing institution. Time and time again they were moved by their pastor's eloquent pleas for contributions; this time was no exception. With one thousand dollars in contributions a house was purchased two miles from up Broad Street. In January, 1892, the Samaritan Hospital opened with a large mortgage still unpaid. It served largely the same constituency as the other two Conwellian institutions.[81]

The refrain was familiar. Conwell was called to do a social service. This time a hospital, a symbol of healing and health, had died. As with Ring, Wiatt, and Davies the woman who asked Conwell to regenerate the hospital could well have evoked the old hurt over abandonment. Conwell responded. He probably had to respond. The Bible was replete with examples of healing. None was more touching than the story of the good Samaritan. Had not the injured man been *left* to die by those who refused to see his need? An old scene surely flashed before his mind. He too claimed he was abandoned dying on the battle-field at Kenesaw Mountain. He had left Johnny Ring and the Newberne command. Then, too, there was the old guilt of leaving family, of seeming better than their legacy. The lesson must not be forgotten; those in need must be attended. The total imagery of the hospital, as the place where people died and were saved, must have reawakened old experiences with particular poignancy. The hurt that abandonment had caused him could not be discarded. Besides, as a civic leader in an era when health was a major issue in city politics, ignoring the need for a hospital was to risk reputation. It was an institution where expertise was needed, drawn perhaps from Temple College his fame as a civic leader would expand. The opportunities for institutional innovation were obvious. In the twentieth century, after numerous additions and the establishment of a medical school, the Samaritan Hospital evolved into the Temple University Medical Center—one of the largest in Philadelphia. The medical staff still remembers the inspiration of its founder.[82]

The future was not as open in the early 1890's as Russell Conwell thought. The Samaritan Hospital was his last institutional creation. The new century would replace the innovator with the administrator as the key institutional personality. It was becoming more important to manage existing corporations and organizational enterprises than to create fresh ones.[83] The shock of the depression of 1893 pointed to the necessary task of ordering the frantic growth of post Civil War America. Conwell did not escape this general shift in orientation. He was forced to exchange his role as an innovator for that of an administrator. But he could not really make the switch. He remained a renovator without the power to effect significant change. The new conditions had important ramifications for his personal predicament.

At Temple the Board of Deacons undertook a policy of institutional retrenchment. In June, 1895, in the midst of a national depression, they met to consider their pastor's request to help relieve the indebtedness of the three Temple institutions through a lecturing tour. Conwell asked leave to travel the lecture circuit for one year. The board was adamant in refusing:

> Resolved, that in view of our past experiences, it has been abundantly proven that the pastor's absence from the pulpit even for one Sunday has always been followed by a decrease in revenues, and we greatly fear if his absence for the extended period of one year was agreed to, many of our pew holders would give up their sittings and the church meet with great financial loss.[84]

The deacons had developed strong reservations about the wisdom of Conwell's institutional creations for the welfare of the church community. Their attitude was considerably less flexible than when they hired the imaginative preacher in 1882:

> Resolved, that we kindly and affectionately remind the pastor that for 12 years his people have born [sic] with the most commendable patience the heavy burdens, and have made great sacrifices to maintain these institutions and have uncomplainingly followed his lead in all the varied undertakings until the strain has become almost unbearable.[85]

They recommended that in order "to save our church and college; that all schemes to enlarge the church, build the hospital or carry on the rescue mission, *or any other work* at

30

present (except what is absolutely necessary) be abandoned." The deacons advised Conwell "to give up much of the work he now has in hand, and give his time only to the preaching of the Gospel . . . and during three days of each week take absolute rest from the awful strain under which he is now suffering."[86] The command to abandon his creative work must have offended Conwell deeply.

The deacons tightened tensions in Conwell that would lead to a nervous breakdown by 1908.[87] Expansion of the Temple institutions had proceeded faster than the capacity to pay. The pastor was continually organizing fairs, subscription and donation campaigns, and lecturing engagements to liquidate indebtedness. The congregation cooperated and thousands gathered to hear Conwell on the road. Still, the buildings were mortgaged and the obligations grew. The deacons became increasingly restive. If he continued to create institutions the money must come from somewhere. For well over a decade he lobbied in the state capital for state aid. Not until 1911 was the legislature convinced that Temple was a non-sectarian institution, and thus deserving of funds.[88] In the meantime Conwell signed personal notes for nearly one hundred and thirty thousand dollars.[89] It was clear that the financial crunch which came to the Temple complex in the two decades straddling the twentieth century was sufficient to lead any man to despair.

Financial pressures, however, did not wholly explain the roots of his breakdown. He started a college knowing that it would take hundreds of thousands to even pay for the new church. The college would drain the struggling church, but he embarked upon the hospital. If Conwell was principally concerned with financial soundness he would hardly have started the college and surely not the hospital. This was not to say he was irresponsible. In travels away from Philadelphia he was acutely aware of even small sums.[90] A more satisfying explanation lay elsewhere; it was to be found in a new dilemma for an old predicament.

As long as Conwell was able to use energies to create institutions which fulfilled public needs he maintained psychic balance. The creation of Christian organizations provided inner adventure while concomitantly connecting him with the abandoned past. The making of the Temple institutions kept his future, i.e., reputation, ambition, and horizons, alive. At the same time these creations reunited him with a past he had fled, dispelling anxiety. They served as arenas in which to act out his hopes and annihilate lingering doubts. As it became more difficult to justify innovation the resolution of these tendencies was rendered remote. In the past whenever Conwell felt the limits of advancement he had either moved or changed roles, often both. As a boy he had left the farm and became a world traveler. In youth he moved out of South Worthington to recruit and later command soldiers. The moves to Minneapolis and Philadelphia also involved role changes. Physical mobility accompanied vocational transformations, which resulted in an enhanced reputation. Indeed, each time he delivered "Acres of Diamonds" in a new town his notoriety increased. Motion delivered fame. But *now he was famous.* People knew of "Acres of Diamonds" by 1900; they were aware of the Grace Baptist Church and Temple College even beyond Philadelphia.

Where could he go for adventure now? What could he do to renew the dreams? There were responsibilities attending the leadership of America's largest Protestant church and its first college designed especially for working people. He was a civic leader. The citizens of Philadelphia would not allow one of their leaders to leave without a stir. A fifty-year-old man could not start anew easily. Restlessness was expected in the twenties and thirties, but bordered on irresponsibility in a man on the far side of middle-age. To leave the church, college, and hospital while they struggled with indebtedness was impossible. His life had continually reminded him of the cost of abandonment. Johnny Ring and South Worthington still haunted Conwell.

But what could be gained in staying? By 1895 the deacons forbade significant institutional innovation. Where was he needed? The whole thrust of his tenure in Philadelphia was that of a builder; others had always run the practical operations. He was the inspiration, the spark for Christian endeavor. In the new atmosphere of entrenchment his usefulness was crippled. The old tension returned in a more agonizing form. He could not leave because of deep-seated self-reproach about abandonment; he could not stay because now no one needed innovation. Before his efforts were always effective, now they seemed superfluous. Worse than that, Conwell's style was actually hindering relationships with his constituency. Later he related to a close associate his frustration with the tightened situation. Regarding some evangelistic work the church was trying to accomplish, he complained that "the people would not come up to our help. The breaks in our work and financial loss to the church discouraged many, and our people are anyhow so dreadfully slow."[91] The balance between creative drives and guilty afterthoughts was being destroyed. The new American desire for consolidation, after the disorders of post war expansion, was expressed not only in the congregation's caution, but in Russell Conwell's malaise. Paradoxically, a man who helped order a rising urban-industrial America was psychologically coming apart.

There were other reasons for Conwell's crisis after the 1890's. In 1901 his daughter Agnes died. The death of his second wife, Sarah, in 1910 continued the heartache.[92] When the century turned Conwell was approaching sixty. From the nineties till his death he suffered periodically from arthritis. He complained frequently and letters show its debilitating effect on his once superb handwriting. It pained him so badly to walk that he occasionally used crutches.[93] This was not the only malady; he spoke of illness of the "motor nerves." As early as 1888 Conwell voiced severe strains. Writing to a niece he lamented, "I do not feel better and am too nervous to write." Expressing a "dreadful lonesome" feeling, he ended with the plea, "I shall soon give out with no help now."[94] By 1910 he referred to being " 'shut in' from all my work by painful illness."[95] Five years later he indicated to a faithful friend that his breakdown in 1908 was not the end of the crisis: "I am greatly discouraged with this strange condition of the motor nerves. But I do not wish to have people know about it as the state of my health is important this year in raising money for the church."[96]

The frequent references to declining health were more than indications of old age. They occurred regularly in his correspondence from the end of his innovational role in the Temple complex. Paradoxically, the decline of Conwell's health was simultaneous with the apex of his personal power. At the very moment when his ability to shape and control the future was the strongest the context of his activities ossified. It must have seemed in the early 1880's that all his struggles pointed toward fruition in Philadelphia. Ten years later the promise evaporated into a holding action. As the years passed the situation took its toll. Conwell not only saw the end of his usefulness, he probably feared the undoing of a carefully cultivated reputation. What if the college closed down? He would take the blame and "Conwell's folly" would become the death knell of a career. All his life people associated bold action with Russell Conwell. Most had marveled at the daring and accomplishment. But there was always an undercurrent of unease. The memory of distraught parents over a runaway boy was undoubtedly dim, but still a part of his old self-reproach. And he could never forget the stigma of a court-martial and dishonorable discharge. He had labored hard to erase that, but now it was possible the entire structure of honor and effort would fall again.

Ailing health and the death of loved ones merely deepened fears about continuing usefulness and the maintenance of reputation. There was mutual reenforcement between illness, grief and the end of an innovational career. The result was much unhappiness throughout the last thirty years of his life. Time after time Conwell would wander back to South Worthington to be nursed back to physical and probably psychological health. During these homecomings did his mind reflect on the wisdom of going to Philadelphia? Was it possible he now consciously questioned a life filled with wandering and restlessness? He was active till the end. He wrote, lived to give the six thousandth "Acres of Diamonds" lecture, and spoke out frequently on public issues.[97] Yet Conwell was a troubled man. A changing America which at first served the needs of his career ultimately held it at stalemate. Intense internal struggles and their resolutions helped create a popular lecturer and the establishment of several important institutions. The openness of post Civil War America with its attending need for institutional growth was a favorable setting for a temporary resolution of Conwell's inner predicament. The saga of Russell Conwell ended its constructive phase with a change in the American environment that was too much for the demands of his psyche. In this sense Conwell's death from cancer in 1925 was anti-climatic: Conwellian creativity had succumbed a quarter century earlier.

His institutions did not crumble. During the thirty-odd years of personal turmoil, doubt, and unhappiness the Temple complex thrived. Temple College evolved into a modern university and Samaritan Hospital, through a superior medical staff, became nationally known. Conwell continued to receive recognition for outstanding accomplishment. In 1922 he received the Bok Award as Philadelphia's outstanding citizen. Rodman Wanamaker entrusted his with the task of writing his famous father's biography. Always he received a multitude of letters from well-wishers inspired by "acres of Diamonds."[98] The reputation so painfully gained and carefully protected remained strong to death. The fears of denouement never materialized. Those who harbored suspicions about Conwell's altruism could hardly quarrel with the final report of his personal wealth:

> An inventory and appraisal of the estate of Dr. Russell H. Conwell filed with the register of wills yesterday shows that the entire estate will not amount to $9,000 after payment of funeral expenses and other charges. As a clergyman-lecturer, Dr. Conwell made nearly $11,000,000 during his life. Yet he left behind him, as an estate, less than one-tenth of one percent of what he earned as minister, lecturer, and author.[99]

The public revered the deceased pastor for the inspiration of his life; the effort and self-sacrifice enacted the noblest ideals of the nation.

Although the outer crust, the reputation, remained untarnished the inner man was frustrated. As Conwell's capacity to shape local institutional life through organizational creation diminished, he grew more anxious. Between 1890 and 1925 in books, sermons, and lectures the texture of an unresolved psychic dilemma was revealed. The content and rhetoric of these writings would show Russell Conwell's crisis in subtle perspective, and mirror American individualism in transit from Victorian to modern values.

References

[1] Russell H. Conwell, *The New Day, or Fresh Opportunities, a Book for Young Men* (Philadelphia: Griffith and Roland Press, 1904), 105.

[2] Arthur Emerson Harris, *Personal Glimpses of Russell H. Conwell* (Philadelphia: by Author, 1949), 16.

[3] Conwell's biographies of famous men devoted a generous space to childhood. A man's beginnings were crucial to character formation. See, Russell H. Conwell, *The Life, Speeches, and Public Services of General James A. Garfield* (Boston: Portland, Maine: G. Stinson, 1881), 1-77. His autobiographical reflections were the foggy ones of old age. He did not accurately recall the correct ages of his parents at their deaths (at least Conwell's recollection was at varience with the ages given on their tombstones). Agnes Rush Burr, *Russell H. Conwell and His Work* (Philadelphia: John C. Winston Company, 1917), 40. See pp. 32-58 in Burr for Conwell's elderly remembrances of childhood. Occasionally he referred to his early years in sermons, but only in dramatic fashion. See Russell H. Conwell, "A Boy Lost," *Temple Review*, XXIV, No. 20 (May 9, 1910), 4-5, Templana Collection, Samuel Paley Library, Temple University, Philadelphia, Pennsylvania; hereafter referred to as TC. There is little "factual" material on Conwell's youth. All existing biographies, including Burr, are romanticized, overlapping, and exceedingly laudatory. William E. Higgins, *Scaling the Eagle's Nest* (Springfield, Massachusetts: James D. Gill, 1889); Robert Jones Burdette, *Modern Temple and the Templors* (New York, Boston, and Chicago: Silver, Burdette and Company, 1889); Albert Hatcher Smith, *The Life of Russell H. Conwell* (Boston, New York, and Chicago: Silver, Burdette and Company, 1899); Russell H. Conwell, *Acres of Diamonds* with *His Life and Achievements* by Robert Shackleton (New York: Harper and Brothers, 1915).

[4] Burr, *Russell H. Conwell*, 29.

[5] For a statistical and analytic examination of late nineteenth century farming see Fred Shannon, *The Farmers' Last Frontier: Agriculture 1860-1897* (New York: Rinehart and Company, 1945), 245-254. William Dean Howell's novel, *A Traveler from Altruria*, gives a perceptive glimpse of the bitterness of late nineteenth century New England farming through the eyes of the character Reuben Camp.

[6] Conwell's grave is on the Temple University campus in Philadelphia.

[7] It is likely that Conwell sold principally wool to Brown who was a wool broker in Springfield. See Burr, *Russell H. Conwell*, 46 and William

36

Robbins Stone, an unpublished and undated biography of Russell Conwell (1910's), 14, TC.

[8] One biographer, a boyhood friend, makes much ado of Conwell's climbs into the Berkshires. William E. Higgins uses one climb Russell made as a childhood omen of future character. See *Scaling the Eagle's Nest*, 7-15. A mature Conwell referred to his home in South Worthington as the "Eagle's Nest" and had personal stationery so embossed.

[9] Conwell quoted in Burr, *Russell H. Conwell*, 16.

[10] This does not mean young Russell was mentally deficient. Higgins observed that although Conwell's teachers found him, "A rather dull scholar when a child . . . yet he seemed to understand books, and in a curious way obtained knowledge speedily." *Scaling the Eagle's Nest*, 27-28.

[11] Conwell quoted in Burr, *Russell H. Conwell*, 68.

[12] The only biography that describes even haltingly Conwell's experiences as a runaway is Burr—but these recollections were Conwell's in his seventies. Also see Conwell, "A Boy Lost," 4-5 for a Conwellian version of being arrested in Paris.

[13] Higgins reported that Conwell worked his way through Wilbraham as a teacher at either Blandford or West Granville (Beach Hill), Massachusetts and by helping Martin Conwell on the farm. *Scaling the Eagle's Nest*, 31. Burr gives the most complete account of Russell at Wilbraham. *Russell H. Conwell*, 90-100. An unidentified newspaper clipping entitled "Wilbraham Attic Yields Conwell's Study Table" (possibly the *Springfield Republican*, 1940's), TC, gives some information on his Wilbraham years. The article notes that Conwell's eye for using the available was exercised at age fourteen when he enrolled his landlord's eight-year-old son in the Old Club Debating Society.

[14] There is no direct evidence of Conwell's parents' ambivalence over their son's growing reputation. But a sermon with a suggestive autobiographical thrust strongly hints that Conwell was aware of the impact of fame on rural citizenry. See "The Country Home," *Temple Review*, XXII, No. 12 (March 23, 1916), 3-7, TC. Conwell talks, for instance, of "this upstart of a boy who once went barefooted down their streets; this boy who could not pass an examination in school; this boy who ran away from home because he felt too large for his neighbors. Now he had come back to overwhelm them. . . .," 4.

[15] One writer sees a connection between Conwell's lean years at Yale and his later hatred of artificial social distinctions. Clyde Nelson, "The Social Ideas of Russell Conwell" (unpublished Ph.D. dissertation, The University of Pennsylvania, 1962), 17. Higgins relates that Russell, too poor to take the regular classical curriculum, was for a time severely ill with a fever, and refused financial aid from the university's administration. He also penned poetry describing his loneliness and yearning for fame. *Scaling the Eagle's Nest*, 31-33.

[16] Elizar B. Hayden to Jennie P. Hayden, September 20, 1862, TC.

[17] Higgins, *Scaling the Eagle's Nest*, 37-38.

[18] *Ibid.*, 44-45. Higgins claimed that this description was made by a critic writing for the *London Telegraph* when Conwell gave an address in 1870 at Leeds, England. The only known recording of Conwell's voice is one of "Acres of Diamonds" given shortly before his death. The record is in the Templana Collection and shows Conwell had a clipped New England accent, but reveals little of his vocal power. A story circulated that Theodore Roosevelt, after hearing Conwell speak, said, "I'd give $10,000 to have a voice like that." Milton F. Stauffer to Nima Conwell Tuttle, April 20, 1943, TC.

[19] Burr, *Russell H. Conwell*, 116.

[20] Russell H. Conwell to Jenny P. Hayden, December 24, 1862.

[21] Joseph C. Carter has recently edited a series of twenty-five of Conwell's letters which were published in the *Boston Daily Evening Traveller* in 1869. See his *Magnolia Journey: A Union Veteran Revisits the Former Confederate States* (University, Alabama: The University of Alabama Press, 1974). These letters are replete with an almost morbid fascination of death, 22-23, 30-31, 76-77, 124. Earlier Carter edited similar letters Conwell did for the *Traveler* on Revolutionary battle sites, "Massachusetts Battlefields of the Revolution," *Daughters of the American Revolution Magazine* (January through April, 1966), 5-10, 98-101, 212-227, 346-349, 424, 437, 442.

[22] This second wound gave Conwell serious trouble six years later because a shell fragment was not removed and worked down from the shoulder to the lung. Burr, *Russell H. Conwell*, 146-149.

[23] The village of Ringville, Massachusetts was full of Rings as a visit to the Ringville Cemetery shows. Miriam Crawford, Curator of the Templana Collection, said she saw Johnny Ring's grave site there. This writer looked but couldn't find the marker. Some markers, however, were illegible.

[24] The Johnny Ring episode loomed large in Conwell's mind the rest of his life. In a visit to Newberne in 1869 he did not mention Ring by name, but it was clear whom he had in mind. Lamenting that "All our old *schoolmates* have fallen in war" he asked, "Was such a *sacrifice* needed? Why does the God of justice permit the men who brought on this fearful War to go free?" Carter, *Magnolia Journey*, 63 [my italics]. Conwell visited New Bern (Newberne) forty-five years later and remarked, "I feel as if the death of Johnny was only last week." Russell H. Conwell to members of the Grace Baptist Temple, July 30, 1914, TC. A Johnny Ring lore has emerged. See Russell H. Conwell, *Story of the Sword* (Philadelphia: reprinted by the Grace Baptist Temple, n.d.) and his *The Legend of Johnny Ring* (Philadelphia: Temple University, n.d.). Conwell's sword hangs in the Templana Collection.

[25] From a photostat of the results of Conwell's court-martial at

Newberne, North Carolina dated May 20, 1864, TC. For a detailed description of the military activities surrounding the dismissal, and reference to his court-martial see U.S. War Department, *The War of the Rebellion: A Compilation of Official Records of the Union and Confederate Armies*, 130 vols. (Washington: Government Printing Office, 1891), Series I, XXXIII, 67-103. Conwell is mentioned on page 69.

[26] What followed Ring's death is still shrouded in mystery and remains controversial. Laudatory biographers have consistently maintained Conwell's innocence. Burr, *Russell H. Conwell*, 125-134, and Robert Shackleton who wrote a biography of Conwell as an addition to Russell H. Conwell, *Acres of Diamonds* with *His Life and Achievements*, 71-75, give the fullest sympathetic accounts of Conwell's military career. Others have undermined his blamelessness and claimed that Conwell's efforts to get his court-martial reversed failed. These critics have also said that the final commission with General James McPherson was, because of the dishonorable discharge, either illegal or non-existent. See Nelson, "The Social Ideas of Russell Conwell," 24-25, and W. C. Crosby, "Acres of Diamonds," *American Mercury*, XIV (May, 1928), 110. It is now clear that Conwell successfully obtained an honorable discharge. The present writer saw the discharge in a gilded frame. Mrs. Marian Sweeny of Springfield, Massachusetts, who now owns part of the Conwell farm in South Worthington, found it. The discharge was dated 1870. Whether Conwell ever served under McPherson or did so illegally is still an open question. Miss Edith Cheney, the late curator of the Templana Collection, investigated the aftermath of the court-martial and found no evidence that Conwell fought in the Battle of Kenesaw Mountain or was wounded. It is significant, however, that *he claimed* to be in battle and left for dead. True or not, he felt a need to find religious conviction in the War experience. See Albert E. Sargent to Edith Cheney, April 11, 1950 (Sargent was the military archivist for the Adjutant General's office in Boston), and Edward F. Witsell to Edith Cheney, June 28, 1950 (Witsell was the Adjutant General of the Department of the Army in Washington, D.C.). Both letters are in TC.

[27] Burr, *Russell H. Conwell*, 132.

[28] Whether Conwell's "guilt" was at its base conscious or unconscious is conjecture. The larger point is that the Ring affair, and its impact on Conwell's view of the past, show the necessity of liquidating self-reproach.

[29] See footnote 24.

[30] The best explanation of the effect of the Civil War on the American mind is George M. Frederickson, *The Inner Civil War: Northern Intellecturals and the Crisis of Union* (New York: Harper and Row, Publishers, 1965). Particularly insightful in describing the changed outlook on institutions is Frederickson's chapter "The Sanitary Elite: The Organized Response to Suffering," 98-112.

[31] These transitional wrenchings are broadly interpreted in book length essays by Robert Wiebe, William Appleman Williams, and H. Wayne Morgan. See respectively *The Search for Order 1877-1920* (New York: Hill and Wang, 1967; *Contours of American History* (Chicago: Quadrangle Books, 1966), 227-488; and *Unity and Culture* (Baltimore: Penguin Books, Inc., 1971).

[32] Conwell married Jenny Hayden in Chicopee Falls, Massachusetts in 1865. Jenny was a friend of Russell's sister Harriet and had been Conwell's student at Wilbraham. She was described as a girl with ". . . a sweet and loving disposition which matched and responded to his own affectionate nature." Burr, *Russell H. Conwell*, 137.

[33] The tension between a longing for a fading rural past and the desire for change which led to wealth and power is made clear in two fine studies of the Jacksonian era. See John William Ward, *Andrew Jackson: Symbol for an Age* (New York: Oxford University Press, 1955); and Marvin Meyers, *The Jacksonian Persuasion: Politics and Belief* (Stanford, California: Stanford University Press, 1957). Also wee Wiebe, *The Search for Order*, especially 11-75 for an interpretation of this strain in the late nineteenth century.

[34] In 1866 Conwell and several others, including Jenny's brother Joseph and a certain "Colonel Stevens," bought into the *Minneapolis Daily Chronicle* which became the *Minneapolis Tribune*. Conwell started and editorially controlled a weekly called *Conwell's Star of the North*. Burr, *Russell H. Conwell*, 140-141. The *Star* not only shows his interest in organizing the G.A.R. and the Y.M.C.A., but also his attempt to propagate "a high standard of morality." *Conwell's Star of the North*, February 8, 1868, Vol. I, No. 1, p. 4. For his work with the Y.M.C.A. see the *Star* editorial, May 23, 1868, Vol. I, No. 15, p. 116. Conwell talked of the "blessed work of evangelizing the world and saving sinners." *Ibid*. The *Star* tried to appeal to a large cross-section of Minnesotans with a "farmer's department," "Ladies' Department," (Jennie wrote pieces for it), "Little Folks Department," and "Temperance Department." The newspaper provided Conwell with the experience of catering to human needs in an urban frontier. He would implement this knowledge twenty years later in Philadelphia.

[35] The health problem emanated from the aggravation of an old war wound. See footnote 22. He was operated on successfully in New York City in 1869 after failing to find relief from hemorrhaging in Europe. Burr, *Russell H. Conwell*, 146-149.

[36] This was the period when Conwell built the reputation of being a world traveler and friend of the renowned. Not only did he augment the ability to talk knowledgeably about places his lecture audiences would never see, but he could tell of visiting Garibaldi, Dickens, Gladstone, Emperor Franz Joseph of Austria, and the Chinese Statesman Li Hung Chang. He never forgot how the first trip overseas had inflated his fame.

See Burr, *Russell H. Conwell*, 151-155.

[37] Conwell's role at the Temple is described in Edgar C. Lane, *A Brief History of Tremont Temple from 1839 to 1950* (Boston: Tremont Temple, n.d. [1950-51?]). His Boston activities in the seventies are best sketched by Burr, *Russell H. Conwell*, 151-169.

[38] Russell H. Conwell, *Life of General U.S. Grant* (Boston: Lee and Shepard, 1872); *Life and Public Services of Governor Rutherford B. Hayes* (Boston: B. B. Russell, 1876); *The Life, Speeches, and Public Services of James A. Garfield* (Portland, Maine: George Stinson & Company 1881). Acclaim for Conwell's writing in the Boston *Traveler* apparently led to a commission to write Grant's biography. Whether this commission came from the Republican Party is unclear. See Nelson, "The Social Ideas of Russell H. Conwell," 43. By 1876 a high ranking Republican, Massachusetts Governor Nathaniel P. Banks, helped convince Hayes that Conwell should write a compaign biography. Nathaniel P. Banks to Rutherford B. Hayes, June 19, 1876. Rutherford B. Hayes Library, Fremont, Ohio.

[39] "Acres of Diamonds" developed from an 1870 publication of Conwell's travel experiences called *Lessons of Travel*. (There is no record of the publisher.) Apparently the genesis of the lecture grew from his observations as a roaming newspaper correspondent in 1870, "The Social Ideas of Russell H. Conwell," 84. From this inauspicious beginning an oratorical monster was produced. Conwell would deliver it over 6,000 times. This meant that if he had given "Acres of Diamonds" daily he could have spoken it every day for almost eighteen years! See Dale Carnagey, "Has Delivered One Lecture 5,000 Times," *American Magazine*, LXXX (September, 1915), 55; Burr, Russell H. Conwell, 313-323; and Robert Shackleton's addition to Conwell's *Acres of Diamonds* with *His Life and Achievements*, 160-170. An interesting portrait of the lecture's success on the Chautauqua Circuit is Victoria Case and Robert Ormond Case, *We Call It Culture: The Story of Chautauqua* (Freeport, New York: Books for Libraries Press, 1970), 61-70.

[40] As early as 1871 there was evidence Conwell was gaining renown. His first biographer quoted the *London Times* referring to the young American as ". . . a writer of singular brilliancy and power, and as a popular lecturer his success has been astonishing. He has made a place besides such orators as Beecher, Phillips, and Chapin." Higgins, *Scaling the Eagle's Nest*, 97-98.

[41] Little is preserved on the circumstance of Jennie's death. Burr indicated that "the rheumatic trouble from which she was suffering went to her heart. . . ." Conwell left her for his work in Boston one morning and returned that evening "to find her dead." Burr, *Russell H. Conwell*, 167.

[42] There is nothing in any of the Conwell biographies to indicate that Russell's and Jennie's marriage was anything but idyllic. Interestingly, Burr described Jenny as "utterly unselfish," a woman who "threw herself wholly into the task of helping him." If Jenny in fact sacrificed her needs

for his, Conwell's self-reproach at her death probably was intense. During their Minnesota years Jenny wrote editorials for the *Star*'s "Ladies Department." Only once did she editorially object to her husband's domination of newspaper policy. After referring to "that cross old fellow having charge of the 'men's department,'" Jenny spoke of the need for equality of the sexes. If one instance reveals a dominating Victorian husband who allowed his wife only tightly controlled expression then the case for grief giving rise to the guilt which often follows the death of a beloved one is strengthened. Conwell's *Star of the North*, May 2, 1868, Vol. I, No. 12, 95.

[43] Burr, *Russell H. Conwell*, 167.

[44] A step-granddaughter described Sarah as "a fine looking woman, patrician-like, rather aloof most of the time, which may have been either tact or indifference." The second Mrs. Russell Conwell "had a lovely smile but used it sparingly," and never allowed anyone to get close to her, "not even her own daughter. . . ." Jane Conwell Tuttle, *Life with Grandfather Conwell and his "Acres of Diamonds"* (South Worthington, Massachusetts: by the Author, n.d.), 10. Also see Burr, *Russell H. Conwell*, 168.

[45] According to Conwell it was the widow, a Mrs. Barrett, who "suggested that I go to Lexington . . . and give an address to such people as might come to the old building." *Ibid.*, 174.

[46] Conwell's Lexington experience is most fully told in Burr, *Russell H. Conwell*, 170-184 and in Shackleton, *Acres of Diamonds*, 76-87.

[47] Shackleton noted that "to have a large and overflowing law practice and take up the ministry at a salary of six hundred dollars a year seemed to the relatives of Conwell's wife the extreme of foolishness. . . ." *Acres of Diamonds*, 85. Burr speaks of Conwell's brother-in-law, Joseph Hayden, as saying he was "dumfounded" by the decision. Burr, *Russell H. Conwell*, 170.

[48] During Conwell's tenure at Lexington (1879-1882) he wrote the campaign biography of Garfield and co-authored with John S. C. Abbot *Lives of the Presidents of the United States of America, from Washington to the Present* (Portland, Maine: H. Hallett and Co., 1882). "Acres of Diamonds" was well-known by the early 1880's because Conwell requested and received permission to *continue* a contract with the Redpath Lyceum of Boston as part of his agreement to accept a pulpit in Philadelphia in 1882. Elliott, *From Tent to Temple, A History of the Grace Baptist Church 1870 to 1895* (Philadelphia: by the Author, 1946), 21. The already popular lecture gained greater acclaim when people learned Conwell was a minister. A critic remarked that "Acres of Diamonds" gained stature because it was "buttered with the authority of a Baptist pontiff." Crosby, "Acres of Diamonds," 104-105. Laudatory biographers agreed that the lecture's "successes" and "inspiration" were the *Reverend* Conwell's contributions. Shackleton, *Acres of Diamonds*, 167; Burr, *Russell H. Conwell*, 313-316.

[49] In 1880 Philadelphia's population was 847,170. By 1890 it had increased over 40 per cent to 1,460,984, although some of the growth was annexation, not immigration. Only Chicago, of those cities of over one million by 1890, increased at a more spectacular rate, moving in the same decade from 503,185 to 1,099,850. New York City's relative gain was less impressive, 1,911,698 to 2,507,414. *U.S. Bureau of the Census, Thirteenth Census of the United States: 1910 Population*, I, 58.

[50] Edward O. Elliott gives an interesting description of a growing north Philadelphia in the late nineteenth century in *From Tent to Temple*, 5-6, 16-17.

[51] The best source for the early history of the Grace Baptist Church and an account of the circumstances of Conwell's employment is Elliott, *From Ten to Temple*, 1-23, Also see Burr, *Russell H. Conwell*, 185-198.

[52] Elliott, *From Tent to Temple*, 21.

[53] Nima was 13, Leon 11, and Agnes 6.

[54] These contradictions are skillfully described in Wiebe, *The Search for Order*, 11-43. Morgan, *Unity and Culture*, 1-74.

[55] Elliott, *From Tent to Temple*, 21.

[56] Burr, *Russell H. Conwell*. Church membership, however, was only 358 in July of 1883. Elliott, *From Tent to Temple*, 32.

[57] When it became known Conwell was thinking about building a new church there was talk of "Conwell's Folly." A theater group anticipated taking over the projected church after its inevitable failure. *Ibid.,* 192.

[58] For various versions of the Hattie Wiatt story see Burr, *Russell H. Conwell*, 197-202; Shackleton, *Acres of Diamonds*, 88-93; and Elliott, *From Tent to Temple*, 33-36.

[59] The depth of Conwell's commitment to building a new church was revealed when some of the congregation intimated that the church was simply a pipe dream. Elliott indicated Conwell said that "unless the church go forward he felt his work was done in this field. The church was very much disturbed at this. . . ." Elliott, *From Tent to Temple*, 38.

[60] For an analysis of Moody's peripatetic evangelism see James F. Findlay, Jr., *Dwight L. Moody: American Evangelist, 1837-1899* (Chicago: Chicago University Press, 1969).

[61] Conwell and John Wanamaker had a long acquaintance, although no correspondence has been located. They were both builders of well-known Philadelphia institutions and each organized Christian activities for the citizenry. Wanamaker wrote the preface for Shackleton's biography of Conwell and described himself as the Pastor's "yoke fellow" and "intimate friend for thirty years." Rodman Wanamaker asked Conwell to write his recently deceased father's biography. An eighty-year-old Conwell agreed. Rodman Wanamaker to Russell H. Conwell, January 3, 1923, Templana Collection. See Russell H. Conwell, *The Romantic Rise of a Great American* (New York: Harper and Brothers, 1924) for interesting similarities in their styles, especially 76-99, 132-148, and 201-219.

[62] A string was attached to the large donation. The money would be deposited to the building fund with the stipulation that the church would be dedicated only when debt free. The string was not honored. When completed in 1891 at a total cost of nearly $210,000 the church still owed approximately $165,000. Only $45,000 had been raised in four years of Conwellian fund raising. Elliott, *From Tent to Temple*, 31, 66.

[63] It was proudly pointed out that the Temple's meeting capacity was greater than the New York and Philadelphia academies of music, and the Music Hall in Boston. Burr, *Russell H. Conwell*, 206.

[64] *Ibid.*, 205.

[65] Thomas Lonsdale, the Temple's architect, was once asked, "What are you doing, Lonsdale, building a fort?" Elliott, *From Tent to Temple*, 60.

[66] Burr, *Russell H. Conwell*, 206. The Baptistry was beneath the pulpit with the organ and the chorus seats behind the speaker. The sanctuary ceiling was fifty feet high. Elliott, *From Tent to Temple*, 63.

[67] When Easter baptismals were performed the pulpit platform was moved backward and the river Jordan was articially recreated. A large pool, rocks, lilies, palms, and "something green . . . like smilax" covered the floor. Then "they turned on the water which came cascading down over rocks through ferns and greenery, lighted by concealed lights. . . ." Tuttle, *Life with Grandfather Conwell*, 74.

[68] Narrations of the Davies story and the beginnings of Temple College are given in Burr, *Russell H. Conwell*, 261-273; Shackleton, *Acres of Diamonds*, 132-147; and Elliott, *From Tent to Temple*, 41-52. Unfortunately there is yet no professional history of Temple College or Temple University, but see Nelson, "The Social Ideas of Russell H. Conwell," 145-201.

[69] Quoted from the pamphlet, "The Temple College. What Is It?" (1888) in Elliott, *From Tent to Temple*, 50-51.

[70] By 1910 Conwell was well aware enough of Rockefeller's endowments to higher education to ask a gift for Temple College. He formed a committee of high-ranking Temple lieutenants to visit President Eliot of Harvard, a member of the Rockefeller Foundation, to ask for funds. Eliot, however, turned down the Temple delegation on the grounds that full public support for the college had not yet been sought. Unpublished letter of manuscript length, Milton F. Stauffer to Millard E. Gladfelter, February 16, 1942, 41-45, TC. Stauffer, who was Temple's vice president and provost in the 1950's, was a member of the committee that visited President Eliot. He helped found the Temple University Association to widen public support for the college. Rockefeller finally did give Conwell a personal check for one thousand dollars, but was annoyed when the latter donated it to the church. John D. Rockefeller to Russell H. Conwell, July 7, 1920, and John D. Rockefeller to Russell H. Conwell, October 10, 1920, both TC.

[71] In 1904 he wrote, "The dangerous tendency to monotony and mediocrity in American life may be in some measure be due to the changed conditions in the occupations of people. Pioneering was once the occupation of all the inhabitants" and men "boldly staked out their future town or farm." But now "new professions and advanced thought are more rarely traits of the American disposition." Conwell, *The New Day*, 103-104. For Conwell "new professions and advanced thoughts" had become synonymous with Temple College.

[72] Dr. Fred Rogers of the Temple University Medical School described an inherited version of Conwell's public relations genius. In every community, immediately after arriving, Conwell asked to see the wealthiest and most influential local citizen. He then promptly asked for a generous donation. Having been invited to speak, with hundreds and even thousands waiting to hear Conwell, the town pillar could hardly refuse to contribute. Conversation with author and Dr. Fred Rogers, Temple University Medical Center, June 18, 1974.

[73] In 1921 and 1922 Conwell gave his last circuit tour for "Acres of Diamonds." The letterhead of the proposed tour read "Russell H. Conwell's Farewell Tour 1921-1922: Acres of Diamonds the $8,000,000 Lecture." Also see Burr, *Russell H. Conwell*, 308-309.

[74] During the early years Temple College's existence depended on utilizing the financial viability of the church, as well as Conwell's lecturing and other money-raising schemes. The church bought the lot to be used for the first permanent college building (Conwell Hall) and transferred the indebtedness to the College Corporation. The church's board of deacons continued haltingly to approve the college's growing indebtedness. By 1895 Temple College held a bonded and floating debt of $109,000. Elliott, *From Tent to Temple*, 84-100. In the nineties Conwell was afraid the deacons would, in their desire to liquidate church obligations, "destroy the college." Russell H. Conwell to Charles F. Stone, January 30, 1892, TC.

[75] There was no state aid in 1911 for payment of the mortgage, purchase of land, or the erection of new buildings. The first state appropriation was $110,000. Stauffer to Gladfelter, February 16, 1942, 48.

[76] When Conwell took a leave of absence in 1908-1909 because of ill health the board tried to reduce his salary from $10,000 to $7,500 per year. Conwell would have none of it. He replied, "I have never accepted dictation by any body of men. I do not propose to accept it now. You will go back and tell the brethren that my salary will remain $10,000." Afterwards it was increased to $12,000. *Ibid.*, 88.

[77] Chief among them was Laura Carnell. Miss Carnell was a Philadelphia girl who studied at the University of Chicago and received Bachelor of Arts and Doctor of Literature degrees from Temple in 1898 and 1902. She was Dean of Temple University Corporation from 1905

until her death in 1929.*Temple Alumni Bulletin*, Vol. 5, No. 3, February, 1939. She personally greeted and helped enroll thousands of college students in the early years. Dean Carnell organized each of the eleven schools of the University. She was known as "Conwell's right-hand man." For an undetermined number of years she lived in the parsonage with the Conwells. Milton F. Stauffer, "The Most Unforgettable Character I've Ever Met" (unpublished, undated [1940's] manuscript), TC. Others of note were Milton F. Stauffer who helped Conwell finance Samaritan Hospital and acted as a kind of financial trouble shooter up until Conwell's death. Stauffer later became Dean of the Business School, Vice President and Provost. During the period 1900-1920 an Assistant Minister Arthur E. Harris and secretary Charles F. Stone relieved Conwell of much routine preaching and personal business. For Stauffer's role see his book length letter to Millard E. Gladfelter and his series of unpublished manuscripts. For Harris check, Arthur Emerson Harris, *Personal Glimpses of Russell H. Conwell* (Philadelphia: Temple University, 1949), and Conwell's letters to Harris, 1912 to 1917. Conwell also wrote often to Stone (1890-1894). All the above materials are in TC.

[78] Besides the steady loyalty of subordinates and the devoted praise of his biographers, Conwell received esteem from the public. Typical of many letters endorsing "Acres of Diamonds" was one insisting that, "that night in 1883 inspired me to continue my fight to gain an education. From 1887 to 1889 I was a student at Millersville State Normal. I won my college degree by four years of hard work." A. Reist Rutt to Russell H. Conwell, October 12, 1921, TC. Another wrote, "Do you know as I read that you had assisted 3,000 college students my heart . . . beat faster and tears flowed o'er my cheeks and I prayed that God might bless you." Lily May Filmore to Russell H. Conwell, September 15, 1921, TC.

[79] At eighty Conwell wanted to start a project called the Greatheart Hospital. No one but him was to have anything to do with its organization. "He wanted to interest entirely new people who were not at work in any other of his enterprises." Stauffer to Gladfelter, February 16, 1942, 36-37, TC.

[80] Conwell quoted in Elliott, *From Tent to Temple*, 76-77. For another explanation of Samaritan Hospital's beginnings see Burr, *Russell H. Conwell*, 288-295.

[81] In 1895 the mortgage and floating debt on the hospital was $13,750. Elliott, *From Tent to Temple*, 100. Two additions were made during Conwell's life time tremendously increasing the indebtedness. Milton Stauffer under Conwell's direction sold more than $3,000,000 worth of bonds at par in 1922 to help Samaritan expand. Milton F. Stauffer (unpublished, untitled manuscript, February 10, 1943), 4, TC. In 1974 Temple University Medical Center began construction on an $80,000,000 general hosptial. Conversation with author and Dr. Fred Rogers, Temple University Medical Center, June 18, 1974.

[82] Dr. Fred Rogers is sure that "Conwell's influence persists" in the Temple University Medical Center. See his *Gallery of Portraits* (Philadelphia: Department of Medical Communications, Temple University Health Sciences Center, 1973), 1-2.

[83] See footnote 31.

[84] Elliott, *From Tent to Temple* , 97.

[85] *Ibid.*

[86] *Ibid.*, my italics.

[87] It is difficult to be precise about the timing of Conwell's breakdown. Milton Stauffer recalled, "I remember when Dr. Conwell had his very bad breakdown when he was 66 years of age." This would be in 1908 to 1909. In Stauffer's opinion (at least the one expressed to Conwell's granddaughter), ". . . his breakdown was due to the fact he was carrying terrific financial burdens." Milton F. Stauffer to Nima Conwell Tuttle, April 20, 1943, TC.

[88] See footnote 73.

[89] Conwell mortgaged his parsonage for $19,000 and borrowed $128,000. Milton F. Stauffer (unpublished and untitled manuscript, n.d.), 8, TC.

[90] For example, he wrote his niece from the fashionable Spencer House Hotel in Niagara, New York: "Be sure you have a complete report of the *number* of delinquents on dues and new rents for the trustees." He urged her to "get it complete in every item." Russell H. Conwell to Agnes E. Hayden, December 14, 1889, TC. Conwell's italics.

[91] Russell H. Conwell to Arthur E. Harris, March 24, 1913, TC.

[92] Strangely, the Templana Collection has no information about the circumstances of their deaths. They did, however, affect him deeply. Conwell wrote a close friend on the fourth anniversary of Agnes' death of being "unutterably lonely." It was after Sarah's death that Conwell became interested in spirit life and told the confidant of his wife's reconstitution: "Every morning at light I see Mrs. Conwell plainly as in the body and she seems to try to answer my questions.   Sometimes it seems too real to be a hallucination and it is too unexpected . . . to be a matter of the imagination." Yet, he concluded, that his visions were probably "a condition of the nervous system." Russell H. Conwell to Arthur E. Harris, December 2, 1914. For a closer look at Conwell's flirtation with the occult see Russell H. Conwell, "Spiritual Telegraphing," *Temple Review*, XXII, No. 10 (January 8, 1914), 3-7, 10. Both in TC.

[93] Russell H. Conwell to Arthur E. Harris, July 31, 1914. Conwell also complained of "the rheumatism in my right side" in a typed letter to Arthur E. Harris, August 22, 1913, both in TC.

[94] Russell H. Conwell to Agnes E. Hayden, July 5, 1888, TC.

[95] Russell H. Conwell to Arthur E. Harris, July 16, 1910, TC.

[96] Russell H. Conwell to Arthur E. Harris, (?), 1915, TC.

[97] For Conwell's views on the Spanish American War, World War I,

and urban and racial crises, see the following sermons: Russell H. Conwell, "America's Danger," *True Philadelphian*, II, No. 13 (June 24, 1898), 347-352; "American Victims;" *Temple Review*, XXIII (May 9, 1915), 3-7; "The Murder of a Policeman," *Temple Review*, XXIX, No. 43 (December 16, 1921), 344-347; and "Colored Migration," *Temple Review*, XXXI, No. 40 (November 30, 1923), 2-8. All are in TC. The best source on the full spectrum of Conwell's positions on public issues is Nelson, "The Social Ideas of Russell H. Conwell."

[98] See footnote 59.

[99] *Philadelphia Inquirer*, February 19, 1926, 8.

2

IN DEFENSE OF HOME

"It is an inspiration to every man to have a home to remember, and consequently, the Lord has taught us—insisted continually—that we should build homes, that a man should be married early, that he should have one home and be happy in it, and that it should be a place next to the throne of God."

> —Russell H. Conwell, *Home Next to Church.*[1]

"Think, if you only had the money, what you could do for your wife, your child, and for your home and your city."

> —*Acres of Diamonds.*

The majority in Conwell's section of north Philadelphia were white Anglo-Saxon, blue collar, working people—many of German descent. In his early years on Broad Street many parishioners came from the country seeking higher wages in the factories of Philadelphia. After World War I the area was fully urban, but many of the congregation remembered the farm. The region retained its white middle-class character until Conwell's death even though it became moderately ethnic.[2] These were the people that sat Sunday after Sunday listening to Russell Conwell. They were the ones he baptized, married, and buried. Temple College and Samaritan Hospital ministered to their educational and health needs. Conwell knew well the people who paid his salary with hard earned contributions and frequently donated to fund-raising schemes, and such a close and lengthy relationship made an impact on Conwell's preaching. For close to a half century the messages were directed to hard-working middle class Philadelphians often vitally involved in the Temple complex. A father who paid tuition to put a son through Temple College listened closely to the college's founder. A mother who gave birth in Samaritan Hospital and sang in the church choir cared about her pastor's point of view. The hopes, dreams, fears, and disappointments of these people were endlessly explored in Conwell's sermons. It was inconceivable that they would have listened for so long had he not been sensitive to their everyday reality.

As a man of national fame, Conwell's weekly talks had the ring of truth. His reputation gave greater weight to sermons aimed at people working diligently to gain a footing in a city and nation often shaking with dislocation. Here was no obscure minister struggling to get ahead like most Philadelphians, but a man who had arrived; someone who had chatted with Lincoln, conversed with Henry Ward Beecher, and was a world traveler. This did not mean Conwell was embraced as a saint who could say anything. Philadelphians, like other Americans, were quick to spot the arrogant, the phony, and the brash.[3] It did mean that when the congregation's mood was sensed and articulated Conwell could both express and guide their feelings. He took his congregation into his confidence and allowed them to see his views were theirs. This was the crucial dialogue, an exchange of confidences. The orations captured the audience because they came from a man who allowed them to see he was genuine. They had agreed to the construction of a church, a college, and a hospital and were not misled; the institutions proved their worthiness. Each Sunday Conwell asked the congregation to consider matters ranging from marriage and death to taxes and censorship. They consistently believed their pastor was right. Conwellian homilies indulged their fears and buoyed their hopes.

One theme seldom failed to fix the attention of Sunday congregations. The refrain was repeated to monotony, but its message never ceased to attract. There was something elemental in its appeal and yet so innocuous that one could listen without offense:

> Dear old home! Do you remember it? Were you born in the country, upon a farm? Blessed indeed is the thought! Do you remember the barn, the cows, the oxen, the horses, the flowers and the old fashioned front yard? If you remember these things, you recall the blessings of God. . . . Oh, just once more to kneel at my mother's knee! Once more to hear my father read the Bible! Once more to sit around the fireside and eat at the old family house and see the playmates of my youth! Oh! To see it, to feel it, to live it once more.[4]

There was "nothing in the world, . . . so influential in reforming the world from sin and wrong as the memory of a good home." Conwell never tired of insisting that a "good home" was "God's great argument." "The memory of home" had no rival "as a measure to tell man what is right."[5] Philadelphians nestled into the red velvet cushioned seats of Temple's sanctuary, gazed at the pastoral scenes in the stained glass windows, and listened to Dr. Russell Conwell's discussions of home.

The message fit the mood. Conwell often began with the modernization of a Biblical story: "This morning an impulse has come to me . . . to parallel one of the most interesting stories in Bible history . . . with a modern instance."[6] On this occasion the parable was the prodigal son. A rich man of country origins, with a "beautiful city home," sat meditating upon his origins. He dwelled upon the contrast between "the homestead on the mountains and this magnificent mansion in the city." Thinking of his boyhood, the wealthy gentleman wistfully thought of the "sacrifices his parents had made for him" amidst the rustic wholesomeness of the old farm.[7] Conwell stirred his congregation's memories:

> Oh, homesick man! Can such a man be homesick who has every honor, who is surrounded with every luxury, who has all the new culture and wealth, whose carriages come to his door, and whose draperies cost more than all the furniture of the old home? Yet, he was heartsick, he was homesick! He could hear his mother call to him; he could feel the clasp of his father's hand at the old gate! Homesick, good man![8]

As the blue-collared audience followed Conwell's delivery they were able to connect the sermon to their experiences. They felt both a traditional middle class envy and distrust of aristocracy and they remembered their own rural beginnings. What hard working factory employee did not, at times, think a greedy city plutocrat was gouging him? Who that could recall did not occasionally wish to be back on the farm? Conwell's sermon promised to be as engaging as the seating was comfortable.

They were not disappointed. The modern prodigal son received word that the old homestead he had reminisced over had burned to the ground. Alas, his dear parents were now living in the barn. The rich man's thoughts turned uncomfortably to his neglected mother and father, to how his own children felt too proud even to visit the old place. But one thought gradually consumed him, "the old home gone."[9] He decided to visit his aging, dispossessed parents. Conwell was in full command of the congregation's interest and he would not lose the opportunity to touch their depths. The homecoming was all the bleeding heart could wish for:

> He rode up the valley, ascended the hill to where, as a child, he always came in sight of the old unpainted barn in which his old parents were living, tears came, and when his old mother came out and clasped him by the neck, and his father took him by the hand, his heart was breaking at the thought of how he had neglected the dear old folks.[10]

Something had to be done. The prodigal resolved to rebuild the house for his parents. Conwell paused to ask the congregation, "Did you ever build a new house for your parents to occupy in their old age?"[11] Many of the brethren probably shifted uneasily. Few could say they had done enough for their parents.

An architect drew up plans for a new house and construction began. All, however, did not go smoothly. The villagers began to gather in small groups and discuss in hushed tones the new house. Was aristocracy going to be established in their midst? Why would a wealthy man from the city build a fine house among poor country people? Suspicions grew. It was rumored an angry mob would burn the unfinished house. Workmen in the area refused to help with the building; they did not want neighbors thinking they were in the pay of city wealth. Labor was imported from the city, but even these men threatened to strike because the few remaining workmen were not union members. Urban riches and pretensions were being embarrassed by common folk.[12] The congregation was finding this story most interesting.

The prodigal was at his wit's end. He had come to do his parents a good turn and was met with wholesale hostility. Work on the house was halted. Everyone urged him to *abandon* it, everyone except his parents. The rich man knew "by their eyes that they wished for their old home." Somehow the house was completed and replicas of the old furniture purchased. The son "had placed it as near as possible like the old home." Magically, a great change now occurred. His pampered children joined him for the house warming. The family knelt in prayer and vowed never again to forsake their parents. They ended the day eating the evening meal in "tearful silence." Early the next morning a carriage came and carried the rich man and his family back to the city; they never returned again. Even so, a message was etched on their consciousness forever: "The house that stood at the corner of the roads" had become "the centre of it all." Conwell closed with an admonition to "write every week to the dear old folks in their old home."[13] Doubtless the north Philadelphia post office was busier than usual that week. Doubtless, too, something stirred in Conwell's own memory.

Conwell repeatedly tried to show that home was "the centre of it all." Once he used the parable of Ruth and Naomi's return from Moab to their old home in the land of Bethlehem. Naomi learned late in life that it had been a mistake to leave the land of her birth for an imagined fortune in Moab. The brethren did not wait long for the Conwellian modernization: "There are some people in Philadelphia . . . who think if they could only move over to New York, or go out west, they would make money."[14] These adventurers would be disappointed because there was "no city in the world that equals Philadelphia for its homeness." To wander in search of greener pastures was no way for a young Philadelphian to find fulfillment. Then Conwell made a point with autobiographical significance, one made in "Acres of Diamonds": "No man is a man until he owns a home. A man who owns his home will be a stronger man, more interested in civic affairs, a better neighbor, and, indeed, a better Christian." He urged even those who were determined to remain single, "to get a piece of land immediately and pay $5 down on it, and $5 next week or next month." No matter how humble the home, a person who owned one had the base to develop "noble character."[15] Love of home simply produced "every possible trait that is worth having."[16]

Conwell would not be misconstrued in the slightest. If a Philadelphian left for "California, or Patagonia or Alaska, and [came] back here fifty years hence," he might be rich or poor, but he would "have lost fifty years of life" and be "an old man."[17] After alluding to several notables, including Marshal Field, John Brown, and Bayard Taylor who returned to their boyhood farms, Conwell delivered the lesson:

> Every man and woman, as he looks back upon life, every man who has had a home; every woman who has had husband and children and home, will find as they look back upon life that that was the ideal point, the highest point of human happiness, and that it was a foolish ambition to do more. God may command man to do some great work; to go out and work as a missionary. But the ideal thing is to own a home, with a wife and children in it, and any single person who has not a wife and children, should have a house or a piece of land of his own, in order that he may, upon that piece of land, worship God and for the strength and confidence it gives every one.[18]

He again ended with the plea, "to write home at once, keep up your correspondence with the old home."[19] Conwell's defense of home promised security in the future and tapped fond memories of the past. There was something personal in his rendering of home which stirred deep hopes and uncomfortable anxieties. Thinking about home engendered an important American ambivalence.

Conwell made the world and home co-extensive; if you understood the latter the former would lose its shapelessness and confusions. Insofar as the congregation grasped homeness they came close to the inner meaning of Russell Conwell's life, and hence to their own. It was a clue of vast significance.

There was an unmistakable relationship between Conwell's idealization of home and his domestic experiences. In an important respect his childhood home was not the "home" to which he later paid homage. The simple fact that he ran away to Boston and to Europe as a teenager hints that he did not find the Conwell household fully satisfying. Life on a poor farm in western Massachusetts, in an age openly seeking social and economic mobility, did not help keep Russell at home. The inability of South Worthington to supply him with "the things that really count[ed]" in the outside world helps clarify young Conwell's flight.[20] For the things that mattered most in the America of the early 1850's were not the stern Puritan reminders about the necessity of hard work, the virtue of thrift, and the earnest religion which Martin and Miranda Conwell tried to imbue in their children. By 1850 the internal dogma of Puritanism had long since disintegrated; control was abandoned for the freedom of various secular and theological adventures. Work was now primarily a means to social and economic mobility; thrift was a way of expanding your credit; and earnest religion was only earnest if it was earnestly enthusiastic.[21]

In short, the spirit of America was open and expansive while the spirit of Conwell's home had seemed closed and constricting. Russell's flight from South Worthington reenacted strains which tore thousands of households apart throughout American history. A liberal ideology and an abundant environment had traditionally broken the cohesion of the American home.[22] Yet with his early act of desertion, Conwell had begun to search for a new model of homeness—a search which climaxed with the creation of the Temple institutions.

Conwell's immediate family was always of great import to him, but a larger family was also a concern. It was not inappropriate to speak of a Conwellian home when one referred to the Grace Church, Temple College, and Samaritan Hospital. Such a "home" sheltered a community which resembled an extended family. The church's community cohesion resulted from the broadly functional and cross-institutional activities of its membership. Conwell, as the institutional father, made sure that the Grace Church was involved in many activities which touched the everyday lives of its parishioners. Whether it was a social function like a church bazaar, charity for the unemployed, hospitalization for the sick, or education of the young, Conwellian institutions were to minister to the needs of its members. A mother and father interacted with their children more personally, but the Temple complex never tired of emulating the more intimate institution.[23] Proximity strengthened paternalism—both Conwell and congregation lived near their church, college, and hospital. For a time in the 1880's and 1890's the situation was analogous to a frontier neighborhood where cooperation and interaction worked to define a community.[24] There seemed little division between Conwell's nuclear home and his institutions as living extensions of it.[25] It is easy to imagine Mrs. Conwell and husband eating countless meals at the church, organizing college social affairs, and endlessly gossiping with church members. The closeness of the relationship became even more understandable when one

55

realizes that by 1900 his natural children were almost grown.[26]

Small wonder that Conwell's sermons emphasized home and family; as the father of a close-knit community, his life was saturated with homeness. His childhood and the emotional shock of losing two wives and a child did nothing to belittle the importance of home. A reputation was carved out of repeated abandonment and restoration of home. The social life of the Temple institutions was a living dimension of a continuing inner saga.

The sermons helped reconstruct the drama, particularly discussions of women and marriage. At the core of home was the character of women and the nature of marriage; the feminine had to be defined and the conditions of wedlock determined. No explanation of Conwell's social fears and hopes, no understanding of his personal crisis could continue without it. Wherever one looked during the Philadelphia years, ladies appeared. A revealing if uncomplimentary view was offered by one of Conwell's granddaughters. The scene was the Broad Street parsonage:

> After dinner came Grandfather's daily nap which he insisted on taking in the sitting room with the ladies all around him chattering as they knitted and embroidered. There were skirmishes over who would take off his coat, who would get the afghan to throw over him, and the prize one, who would stroke his forehead until he fell asleep. Only a few people thought he ever really slept during the naps. It was a fine chance to get material for sermons and also bits of juicy gossip. . . . You may well ask "where was Mrs. Conwell while the nap and hen party were going on?" Well, she was there, serene,—I won't say untroubled, but above it all. She had no doubt, resigned herself to having all sorts of women around by this time, but I still believe it disturbed her.[27]

Often weddings were held in the parsonage. "Grandfather kissed the bride loudly" and took payment for the ceremony unless, "the bride was young and pretty." If so "she got the fee back." The granddaughter speculated, "I hate to think what a Don Juan he might have been" had he not been a minister.[28]

Conwell's interest in young ladies also occurred in sermons. Young Philadelphia gentlemen were told that "the woman whom you can love as a home-maker must be a person whose mind will be wholly enveloped in that home."[29] The prospective bride "should be feminine, not masculine, sweet, dainty, tender, affectionate and conscientious" and unless she was all these, "she will not be true to you." Even a Victorian could at times be blunt: "You would not marry a woman with a club or a gun. You should marry a woman whom you must protect, who will be dependent upon your protecting power. You must not marry a woman who is too independent of that." They were to beware of women who were "running to men's business!"[30] The matter bespoke of intimate role insecurity which beset the era.[31]

Divorce was the obvious menace to home and hence to womanhood and marriage. It was inimical to the deferential home and hence to fundamental role identifications. Conwell had strong feelings on the subject: "The most dangerous thing in society, the most efficient weapon the devil wields, is the weapon of irreverence for the marriage relation."[32] Divorce destroyed the home as a superior social model and ushered in a host of crimes. Christian civilization would face "awful dangers" if marriage was endangered.[33] The spector of abandonment which divorce presented likely reopened Conwell's inner struggle. It was a highly visible reenactment of the dilemma of desertion so close to the meaning of his life.

Conwell believed that the problem of divorce was really centered in the nature of marriage. Divorce was frequent because young people often began marriage without genuine union. Only when the sublime nature of merger between men and women was realized could marriage be marriage. The first mistake many couples made was in thinking that an authentic marriage was the formal ceremony. "Real marriage" was in "the motive" and not in the "outward contract."[34] A covenant between pure hearts was essential. Young people who lived together without being married in spirit were cohabitating in a "continuing crime." The remedy was not stricter divorce laws. Disunions should be "more easily obtained than they are now, save for the salutary effect of punishment." If the courts found the character of the man to be debased then his wife was entitled to a divorce; the reverse was also true. "Evidence of fornication . . . in character" was enough to end the outward pretense of an inner union never made.[35]

Without pure marriages a proper defense of home could not be maintained. And, without men and women who scrupulously guarded their characters (i.e., their sexual identities), the Victorian world would unravel. By sharply defining women and marriage Conwell could focus the outlines of his psychic predicament. The obligations toward a remembered home would remain meaningful only if a sharp picture of its ideal qualities were maintained. Harbored guilt about leaving an early remembered home could be channeled successfully because home was perceived in lofty terms. Distinct notions of sexual roles and domesticity meant more than anxiety about a changing America. They hinted at the necessity of embracing Victorian values. The self-incrimination and tension this creed engendered was essential to its preservation.[36] Again, Conwell's idea of womanhood was instructive, for its very ideality was rooted in the need to see it threatened.

Consider his interpretation of Mother's Day. Conwell removed any doubt about the importance of mothers to mankind: "The study of the philosophy of history, which has become a very deep and well-founded science, shows that nearly all, . . . the great geniuses of the world inherited special gifts from their mothers."[37] He looked back introspectively to his boyhood in South Worthington:

> I remember as my mother's boy—I was her youngest—how she encouraged me, how she overlooked my weakness, and how she prayed with me. On the other hand, I remember my father had a switch—two or three—of the very hardest ironwood, and whenever I did wrong and he knew it, that switch was to come down and I was to feel it—hard fierce justice, combined under all with a tender love. If I hurt myself, did I run to my father? No, it was to my mother I went that she might kiss away the pain. You did the same. We are alike in human nature.[38]

As he confided domestic secrets to the Temple congregation he exposed a major source of Conwellian strength. People knew when they were told that "the great men of the world" inherited the ideas and "moral purposes of the mother" that it was true; they were listening to a great man for whom it was true. Many probably thought of their own mothers, some with pride, some with sorrow, but all with a measure of anxiety. Would they have been great if mother had been more saintly, or did the fault lie within themselves? Had they treated her well? Conwell was sure that throughout "the history of mankind" a boy was "what the mother makes him." If there was wickedness and "dishonesty in high places" it was due to "mother's teaching." The home was the "throne of power" for mother; it was there that man's character was charted—for better or worse.[39] Mothers defined masculinity. The thought generated as many qualms as it squashed.

But the occasion was for mothers. Conwell announced that "the mother holds a place next to God" and if "a woman . . . falls into sin" she was "more vile, degraded, and hell-like than a man ever can be." Yet there was a Victorian refuge. When a lady stayed "in the home in a normal condition as a mother, she seems next to God." There, "no knife [could] draw the line between the love of mother and the love of Christ."[40] What strains stretched taut in women who had pampered themselves instead of their brood were conjectural; but those in single girls, unwed mothers, or divorcees were obvious.

Who would leave the Temple for the streets of Philadelphia with an entirely clear conscience? Who would not be more convinced than ever that for a man to be manly the virtues of true womanhood must be preserved? What woman could live up to Conwell's ideal? Anxieties festered while resolutions to do better were contrived.

In 1898 at age fifty-five Conwell wrote a novel which was never published. "Out of the Floods" amplified many Conwellian ideals but none more starkly than defense of home and true womanhood.[41] The story was probably never publicized because it was baltantly autobiographical; Conwell might have been accused of self-indulgence. The novel showed that the sermons on domestic life and proper sexual roles were not just topics shrewdly calculated to fill the church; these themes encompassed internalized values which lay at the heart of Conwell's personality. There were some things even a popular man could not popularize. Even so, they proved not in the least a disjunction from his public pronouncements: "Out of the Floods" made Conwell's language and inner tensions seem of one piece.

The novel was set in the happy time before the Civil War, when ideals seemed clear and evil easily identifiable. The plot was unembarrassingly romantic. Even the dullest reader could see the eternal struggle between good, beauty, and truth on the one side and evil, ugliness, and error on the other. Caleb Warder, the handsome and heroic but wandering young man, began the action with his arrival in a small town somewhere in western Massachusetts. A stranger to the area, he sought out his only living relative, an old character named Uncle Palm. Shortly thereafter Caleb was accused of the brutal axe-murder of his elderly uncle. While in prison awaiting trial, he received moral and legal aid from two paragons of feminine virture, Sarah Maria Smith and Bessie Otis. Though the latter's testimony saved him from hanging, the town's lingering suspicions forced Caleb to flee Massachusetts and begin a new life in Iowa. After changing his name and studying law the young wanderer ran for political office on the anti-slavery ticket. Caleb quickly became a leading frontier citizen, all in sharp contrast to the earlier restlessness. The new sense of purpose resulted from the evangelizing efforts of Sarah Maria and Bessie who had followed Caleb to Iowa. There, Uncle Palm's real murderers, who earlier had swindled Sarah's father's property, kidnapped both girls. The abductors abused and overworked their captives, thus causing Sarah's death. But Conwell was quick to show her demise as a victory for Christ. The feminine martyr's last moment brought a vision of ascension. Besides, Bessie escaped after Sarah's death and was eventually united with her soul-mate, Caleb. The couple returned to Massachusetts to apprehend the villains who had fled from Iowa. They were too late to apply human justice; God intervened with a flood which not only dispatched Uncle Palm's murderers, but providentially unearthed the old man's hidden treasure which, of course, now belonged to Caleb and Bessie. All ended satisfactorily for hero and heroine who were convinced that people with genuine moral qualities could achieve the goodness, love, and self-improvement necessary to conquer the most dastardly evil.

"Out of the Floods" was clearly in the tradition of the Victorian novel rather than the emerging realist school. There were not only clear-cut models of male and female but sharp categories of good and evil. The novel never hinted at the possibility of relative truth; absolute values reigned supreme from start to finish. Although there was never any doubt about who the good and evil characters were, good people did have weak moments. Caleb went through a great deal of self-incrimination before he achieved sure knowledge of the good. What emerged was a lesson for life, a story with absolute moral meaning and deep autobiographical tone. The didactic elements established themselves early and were sustained to the end—in this it differed little from Conwell's published writings.[42] Doubt, ambiguity, and contradiction were neatly cut away and yet anxieties remained, tensions essential to the creation of Victorian simplicities. Without vexation no moral allegory could unfold—neither could Conwell's inner dilemma.

Parallels between Conwell and the novel's hero abound. They were both wanderers as young men. Each went west to start a new life. Both were peoples' lawyers and visualized themselves as self-taught, if not self-made. Both were publicly accused of an unmanly crime—Conwell of desertion and Caleb of the murder of an old man. Each felt officially innocent of the charges. Each had flirted with atheism and was temporarily consumed with self-doubt. Conwell had agonized over his dishonorable discharge while Warder was filled with remorse over a life wrongly lived while he was jailed for Uncle Palm's murder. The death of a young woman had profoundly affected each—Caleb by Sarah Maria Smith and Conwell by Jennie Hayden. Interestingly, even the names of the influential laides were not very dissimilar—Bessie and Sarah for Warder and Jennie and Sarah for Conwell. Most important, in each of their lives a crucial trauma occurred after they realized someone had sacrificed something dear for their moral uplifting. Johnny Ring's death brought into Conwell's consciousness festering doubts over abandonment of home and God. Caleb felt guilty after recognizing that his best friend in Iowa, Parson Gunnison, had sacrificed love for Bessie Otis upon learning of Caleb's own amorous feelings. Was Conwell remembering an old personal wound when he described Caleb's reaction to Parson Gunnison's generous self-denial:

> I'm lost! Lost! Lost! I deserve the hell I am in, and have myself made the perdition I shall be in hereafter. If God and my friend will only forgive me I will give up all. I will never take what my friend offers [Bessie's love]. I ask nothing but forgiveness. A crust of bread and a pure heart is all I ask. I want nothing but to be a better *man*. But that can never be. Never.[43]

Did guilt help both to discover what it took to become men in a Victorian world?

The meaning of religious conversion was also roughly parallel. It was after Johnny Ring and Kenesaw Mountain that Conwell decided to be active in the cause of Christ. Likewise, after Gunnison's sacrifice Caleb was convinced that "he would devote himself hereafter to the work of making everyone else happy and doing all the good he could crowd into the remainder of his life."[44] Both post-conversion lives were absorbed by crusades. Caleb used his self-taught law to enter the political campaign against slavery, just as Conwell used his organizational talents for Christian causes in Minneapolis, Boston, and Philadelphia. Significantly both Warder and Conwell had their crucial religious awakenings in a younger America, a world taken with the idealism of ante-bellum values. Here was an environment where manhood and morals meant fulfilling Christian action. When the setting of the 1890's made the resolution of familiar anxieties more difficult, he could at least abate them through an imaginary character—one with suspiciously similar psychic tensions. The place of women and home in "Out of the Floods," however, showed that Conwell was unsuccessful in fully displacing anxieties. An elemental cultural strain remained.

The clash of two feminine wills symbolized the struggle between good and evil which pervaded the novel. Early in the story Caleb was asked to judge a local debate on the question of women's rights. One side of the issue was presented through Miss Sally Ann Thompson who later married the French aristocrat Julian Vernet, the arch-villain and real murderer of Uncle Palm. Sally's character was conveniently revealed in her physical appearance:

> She was about twenty-eight years of age, and so tall that she stooped to clear the door. . . . Her mouth was sunken like her eyes, and one tooth had disappeared from the upper row. Her general appearance was of a manish woman . . . filled with chronic indignation that she was not born a boy.[45]

The incongruity of a "manish woman" forewarned of Sally's demand for male-like political and economic power. It also hinted at Conwell's uneasy awareness of the era's shifting sexual roles. Ironically, masculine designs and aggressiveness seemed to be creating manish women. A more assertive America threatened traditionally passive female roles. Sally's arguments embodied the contradiction. She attacked the conventional vision of womanhood: "Woman! What is a woman but the slave of man? Woman! Noble woman! What hast thou had for all ages but toil and pain? What bread hast thou eaten, save such as stingy man has doled out to you in dribblets?" Male behavior left much to be desired as "hard-hearted man, has spread his broad palm over the hills and said 'these are mine'." He had "spread his broad palm over the seas" and claimed them as well. Acquisitive man "piles his wealth in banks, and enriches himself in speculative stocks . . . but woman, where is she?"

Miss Thompson's answer was devastatingly simple, ladies were "only the tail of his kite." But men could not continue to consume female identity with masculine power:

> If false and cowardly man dares refuse your petition hurl him to his doom! Let the woods be peopled with seekers after vengeance; let the highways become dangerous, and the fields but places of execution! Let horrid murder haunt him by night and fearful assassination startle him at noonday, until woman shall be wholly free. . . .[46]

Here was a blunt threat to nineteenth century manhood and all the security it assumed. Here too was a source of anxiety elemental in urgency; one calculated to make men cling to a Victorian world. If women were allowed to cut away the male-dominated past, the safety of Victorian identity, and the past as the remembered generator of that identity were menaced. But the force of Sally's threat was even more encompassing for it involved a massive undermining of the inner dynamics which created Conwell's reputation. Behind his post Civil War self-reproach was the assumption that it could be assuaged through reestablishing origins, by going back home. If women became men, or usurped male functions, they confused "homeness," the quality which engendered guilt—without which Conwell could not have forged his reputation. He had to keep this anxiety, a task which was becoming more difficult in an urban-industrial environment bent on reducing traditional identities to the needs of modernity.

What Sally loathed and what Conwell was simultaneously attracted to and guilty about was man's freedom to conquer the environment and to grasp in the process wealth, power, and reputation. Those were also the very things she would kill to get. She emulated what Conwell thought was worst in man and most troubling about himself. Sally was the image of the most rapine, self-seeking avaricious late-nineteenth century American male imaginable. Much worse he happened to be a she. Miss Thompson was the ultimate threat. Once the drive for power infected womanhood man stood in grave danger. Masculine feminity threatened Conwell's vital center; the home with all its metaphoric and inner meaning would crumble. Sally was a creation evil enough, frightening enough, to project and yet absorb deep personal anxieties. If he was unable to continue to reconnect with the past through channeling culpability into the construction of homelike institutions someone must take the blame. Sally was the perfect foil. Strains which threatened to undo a lifetime of carefully calculated personality integration needed release. The creation and then destruction of a monstrosity representative of subterranean levels of doubt and psychic anxiety could provide some relief. The paradox was there also; the female threat to masculine culture was bound to produce more intense tension. Conwell needed what he loathed and loathed what he needed.

Only a vision of ultimate good could effectively oppose such an insidious character as Sally Ann Thompson. Sarah Maria Smith served admirably. Her inner beauty gave every confidence of being the antidote to the poisonous Sally:

> What a sublime thing is a pure loving woman! Nothing else in art of nature approaches the majesty and delicious sweetness of a cultivated stainless woman! Such a woman was Maria Smith. She was not externally beautiful as Bessie, but Maria had a stronger will, a deeper heart, and a more brilliant intellect. . . . It would have required the form of Juno to have matched the mind and soul of that country maiden, Maria Smith.[47]

There was nothing in Sarah Maria's argument to disturb the vision. She understood pure feminity. Maria responded calmly to Sally's invective: "It [was] delicious and grand to be a woman" because God had not intended females "for camps and sieges, battles and marches."[48] Gazing squarely at Sally, Maria attempted to eliminate any confusion about where genuine female identity was to be found:

> The holiest nook in all God's universe, and the most blessed situation is the quiet retirement of a cultivated home. That is a woman's birthright and no man or woman has a right to drive her forth to uncongenial, unwomanly work and publicity. Let

the men be men. . . . Woman—true, pure and holy. Woman—sweet, white and beautiful. Woman—honest, earnest, and faithful. Woman—loving, tender and patient. Woman—modest, retiring and Christian. . . . I claim the right to be a woman.[49]

What else could she have said to blunt Sally Ann Thompson's argument? There was only one place where a lady could find a stable identity. The very place young Conwell had tried to abandon could restore the role security he and others of the era needed. The one refuge from involvement in the disorders and impersonalizations inherent in the modernization of an agrarian society was the American home and the values it nurtured. Home and the lost pastoral past seemed one.[50] To defend women-in-the-home was a way of reasserting remembered inner obligations; a domestic bulwark filled with virtuous females was a psychological anchor in an America which seemed as out-of-joint as Sally's argument. Without a massive defense of "home," Conwell's personality threatened to become as unraveled as national life.

The tenacity with which Russell Conwell held to his ideal of home exposed a major tension in his social assumptions and pointed to a broad cultural malaise. Since it was frequently necessary to emphasize the preservation of domestic values and traditional identities, Conwell must have elaborated upon the symbolic threat—Sally Ann Thompson—publicly. And, he did. Conwell believed that society, between the Civil War and World War I, was a society "over-reaching" itself. If more polite than the anxieties Sally evoked, his qualms about "overreaching" nevertheless constituted an apprehensiveness which reflected a wider unease.

Conwell gave two meanings to overreaching which showed two major misgivings in an era of gigantic historical transition. One import revealed a distrust of selfishness. He had trepidation about the naked pursuit of something without regard for social and spiritual considerations. He warned the Temple congregation to be wary of the man who over-estimated his value. Christians had best beware of "the man who claims from society more than he is worth," for this was a man "who over-reaches his neighbor." Self-assertion was, however, still desirable. Philadelphians were not to underestimate themselves and become "Uriah Heeps." True humility was the art of recognizing oneself "at his true valuation—not one iota added or taken away." He warned that "sinful selfishness begins where truth and equity and love cease."[51] His life disclosed that the balance between selfish ambition and community obligation had deep inner meaning. Yet the plea for moderation, of needing "to know exactly to the penny what you are worth" assumed another kind of "overreachingness," one which menaced community values. Conwell was certain that "half of the world is going on in that financial dream" and unaware of "the actual condition of their finances."[52] To the end of his life he believed that "steady, permanent advance is much better . . . in business than in any sudden speculation . . . which overloads a man with responsibility and anxiety."[53] On the personal level this was ironic given the financial risks he took in creating the Temple institutions. Still, there was a broader concern in his caution.

The second rendering of overreachingness clarified Conwell's idea of selfishness; it was directly related to his uneasiness about America's great economic and social transition. The problem was the growth of financial machinery which got beyond the control of individual responsibility. A society which depended on impersonal processes rather than on personal contact in conducting daily business was an "overreaching" society. In 1893, a year when this development seemed politically explosive, Conwell posed some timely but discomforting questions to the male members of the congregation: "I ask all these experienced men here . . . have you gotten your money dishonestly? Did you secure it by unfair means, by overreaching other people? Have you oppressed the widow, the orphan, the poor, to obtain your money?" There must have been some nervousness in the pews. Conwell uncompromisingly assured those that had "overreached" that they would never "sleep in peace." He wanted business which undertook, "in an honest way to deal with . . . fellowmen, and supply what they need fairly and squarely."[54]

Unfortunately, modern business machinery increasingly prevented the personal contact which seemed necessary for honest dealing and honest profit. Nationalized banking and distended marketing generated a need to retain villagelike business.[55] Undoubtedly many remembered a smaller rural world where selfishness was more properly contained. Conwell's guilt continually revealed a remembered obligation to the older

66

setting. There, roles were more easily discernible, and mutual trust a rule of thumb. The transparent paradox was that the "experienced men" Conwell addressed, which included himself, had become "experienced" through abandonment of the personalized world they recalled. But why did they continue to listen to a man who came close to incriminating their life styles? Conwell was scratching at the tip of a troubled American psychological iceberg. Nothing testified to this submerged crisis as well as the sustained popularity of Conwell's most famous lecture. Here his inner struggle and their psychic situation found the most dramatic common ground.

American historians have remembered Russell Conwell, if dimly, as the creator of "Acres of Diamonds." They have dutifully reported the gist of the lecture as a materialistic pastor's insistence that every man in America had a God-given duty to get rich. The fact that Conwell delivered "Acres of Diamonds" thousands of times for over fifty years only confirmed how slavishly Americans of the Gilded Age clung to the doctrine of individual opportunity. It was quite typical to embrace the hope of individual advancement in an age when corporatism was rapidly undermining its reality. This explains the frequent generalization that "Acres of Diamonds" exemplified an older American tradition resisting momentous economic and social change. The judgment was correct, but too simple. And, this insight was subsumed within a larger interpretation of the Gilded Age which assumed that the Conwells and Horatio Algers were prime examples of the period's predominating aggressive materialism.[56] True, the popular mind still guided itself by Jeffersonian-Jacksonian expectations of economic and social mobility. Without the image of "the man on the make" the era would be incomprehensible. But the interpretation is one-dimensional and hence misleading. A different reading of "Acres of Diamonds" illuminates a more complex mood, one complicating the standard view of the era.

Victorian beliefs put easy "man on the make" assumptions in a new perspective. Many Victorian values were the very antithesis of the ambitious materialistic Jacksonian ones. The Victorian frame of mind gave great weight to the qualities of moral integrity, respect for self-sacrifice, heroism, romantic love, and sanctity of past and place. In an age which seemed more than any other to be disregarding these verities, insecurity was everywhere. As traditional moral anchors were cut adrift in a rising sea of normative relativism little wonder reassurances were sought.[57] Perceived as an anchor to secure a society floating in intellectual, economic, and social drift "Acres of Diamonds" shows a different American predicament. The lecture's title is revealing. From the Victorian angle, "Acres" suggested something quite dissimilar to limitless American space. Instead, "Acres" became circumscribed place, one with more than a modicum of sanctity and permanence. A closed frontier could be as restful as it was exciting. Then, too, "Diamonds" were a gem of incredible hardness, a stone impervious to destruction. As old ways crumbled a symbol of immutability attracted. Finely cut "diamonds" refracted light beautifully and reminded many of the sanctity of marriage. Diamonds and marriages were supposed to last forever, just like the nostalgia for remembered homes set in a pastoral America. Surely one could shut out, for a time, the unpleasant confusions of the day in the midst of "Acres of Diamonds." Such a notion does not deny the lecture's title as a symbol of great wealth. Rather wealth itself could rescue one from misgivings about the pervasive and ceaseless striving which saturated American life. Wealth gave men identity and place in a society bent on destroying both. "Acres of Diamonds" could circumscribe and preserve a Victorian setting. It complimented the era's fixation on the ornate and ponderous in architecture and clothing—obvious attempts to find imperturability within ubiquitous American change.

The meaning of the lecture was as much a native hope for security as a desire for God approved materialistic opportunity. An overpowering need for security was grounded in a yawning national insecurity which stretched back to the jeremiads of the Puritan fathers. A gnawing unabated feeling that the development of America had somehow gone askew was never far from the surface. Countless Fourth of July orations which colored the national past in idyllic shades bespoke of a premonition of the opposite. Various reform endeavors and national crusades expressed the discontent, but anxieties often remained unreleased. The average citizen, as Henry David Thoreau observed, lived a life of quiet desperation while carrying out the business of transforming America into an even more disquieting place. Conwell's inner struggle was a melodramatic rendition of a wider unease. Why did Americans flock for half a century to hear "Acres of Diamonds"? He, they, and the times shared a significant intimacy.

Conwell began by repeating a story he said an Arabian guide passed on while the young correspondent was traveling in the Middle East in the late 1860's. The essence of the guide's tale, reiterated in a dozen different ways in the lecture, touched a common predicament. After describing the misery wrought to one prosperous Middle Eastern farmer who left a pleasant life in search of "a mine of diamonds," Conwell made the crucial point:

> Had Ali Hafed remained at home and dug his own cellar or his own garden, instead of wretchedness, starvation, poverty, and death in a strange land he could have had for every acre, yes for every shovelful of that old farm . . . the gems which have decorated the crowns of monarchs.[58]

The passage, like many others in the lecture, justified the acquisition of material wealth as a desirable human goal. But always one's own home, cellar, garden, or farm were the most appropriate places to seek wealth. Conwell's warning of unhappiness and destruction for those who sought riches beyond their own locale exposed an important contradiction between conceptions of ideal homes and the reality of a distended America. Emerging modernization had fragmented thousands of American homes and made the defense of domestic values more urgent. This outcropping hinted at a darker dilemma. The message was autobiographical on a vast scale.

The meaning of America was entangled in its need to move. A peripatetic society was born in movement from Europe and developed amidst a multitude of wanderings. Restlessness had peopled half a continent and was now engaged in building a colossal urban-industrial national identity. The new forms seemed at variance with the shape of an earlier era, and it became more difficult to accept their common substance— restless movement. The result was an acute anxiety about the legitimacy of the emerging national style. The populist outburst of the 1890's was only an exceptionally dramatic seething of massive discomposure. The broader implication suggested that escalating national restlessness served the psychological needs of the coming of modernity. The key to continued American development was to direct native unease toward continued growth, not as the Populists wanted, to dissipate it in counter-productive political hyperbole. "Acres of Diamonds" generated all the guilt and foreboding necessary for growth and channeled them into orderly shapes. Insecure backward-looking feelings were not useless to, but used by, the new America.

Conwell and his America were engaged in resolving native anxieties which threatened to get out of hand. Of those who listened to the lecture's instance after instance of disastrous wanderings and successful homecomings, who could not see the same pattern in themselves? Who had not moved to a new town, only to hear later of a wealthy neighbor who had stayed at home? Who had not moved to a new town, grown successful, and wondered if he had not lost more than he had gained? Childhood beginnings always generate the need for independence but the American environment provided the setting for extraordinary wanderings; the basis for later unease was buried in everyone's infant past and in a forever restless American present. Conwell's famous message was no less than the mirror of an Americanized Oedipal pageant—one which avoided, in typical Victorian fashion, any overt offensiveness. "Acres of Diamonds" told enough to continue generating native anxieties, but not enough to face an important question squarely: Americans were compelled to kill their beginnings if they wanted a powerful future. Instead, they were told if they did not stray from their origins they could preserve the past and own the future. Adventure and security were the same thing, at home. If they did not sever the cord they could develop confidence in wealth and reputation. What Conwell's guilt proved untrue, thousands of Americans seemed to swallow whole.

"Acres of Diamonds" worked. Inner tensions were soothed at the very moment new ones effervesced. Somehow people knew that the hypnotic voice and relevant message of the "successful" Russell Conwell captured a special part of themselves. In booming tones he told them that "never in the history of our country was there an opportunity so great for the poor man to get rich as there is now...." No one should despair, for "the very fact that they get discouraged" was "what prevents them from getting rich."[59] This was what America was all about, and it certainly was what they hoped and dreamed.

Everyone at times faced discouragement, but they knew what Conwell said rang true: to give up and stop striving was fatal. Here was a man of reputation telling thousands to keep up their restless, never-ceasing ambitions. If they did, they, like him, would find "Acres of Diamonds." All the toil and trouble would be worth the effort. Or would it?

Conwell ended the famous panegyric with a troubling challenge, one failing to put his audiences at ease:

> He who can give to his people better streets, better homes, better schools, better churches, more religion, more happiness, more of God, he that can be a blessing to the community in which he lives . . . will be great anywhere, but he who cannot be a blessing where he now lives will never be great anywhere on the face of God's earth. [60]

Those who felt that ambition was the answer to all of life's vexations were disappointed. Unless striving was coupled with community improvement, happiness proved illusory. The connection between Conwell's life and the American experience became clearer. They were listening to a man who had struck it rich at home. He was making Philadelphia a place of "better homes, better schools" and "better churches" and he was richer because of it. Who amongst Americans could say the same? What man or woman could dismiss the life of Russell Conwell as unimportant? He had resolved the anxieties over abandoning beginnings through channeling them into the construction of home-like institutions. They wished, unconsciously or consciously, to do the same. The message of "Acres of Diamonds" told them how to ease their unease; Conwell's life of home-building would be their guide. The autobiographical thrust of the lecture was unmistakable. Conwell lived his lecture. Who that heard it could do the same? Disquietude remained.

The American public wanted to do what was right. They also wanted the success—a quality to be achieved by abandoning their father's ways. "Acres of Diamonds" played to, and upon, two deep-seated national characteristics, the need to feel morally justified and the desire for power and wealth. Two such incompatible aspirations could never be successfully resolved. Yet the lecture attempted such a synthesis. Russell Conwell's life was a living model of the compatibility of self-interest and community spirit. Nevertheless, Conwell suffered a nervous

71

breakdown. It seems plausible his collapse was related to the strain of pursuing two disparate goals at once. In attempting a rapprochment between materialism and idealism "Acres of Diamonds" excited hopes while simultaneously activating forebodings that the synthesis could not be made. The human predicament had been cast for countless Americans in a setting which exaggerated inescapable childhood strains. A milieu which encouraged abandonment as a prerequisite for personal success generated vast quantities of anxious energies which were channeled into the building of modern America. The popularity of "Acres of Diamonds" accented the meaning of home in Conwell's life. Thousands saw the reflections of their own hopes and fears in an allegory of one man's inner contradiction. They hoped his solution could be theirs.

The late nineteenth and early twentieth centuries felt the full force of the incongruities of modern life come to America. The energy of a society immersed in transformation demanded that the old verities be forsaken with a force unequaled in the national past. Even the security of domestic sexual roles seemed uncertain. What was to take the place of disintegrating patterns? Conwell's sermons reveal more than the depths of native fears about home; they illuminate an American style of institution-making. Here unfolds yet another implication of Russell Conwell and the crisis of American individualism.

References

[1] Russell H. Conwell, "Home Next to Church," *Temple Review*, XXVI, No. 11 (February 24, 1918), 5-TC.

[2] Elliott, *Tent to Temple*, 5-6. For newer accounts of the Philadelphian atmosphere in the late nineteenth century see Sam Bass Warner, *The Private City: Philadelphia in Three Periods of Its Growth* (Philadelphia: University of Pennsylvania Press, 1968), and Allen F. Davis and Mark Haller, eds., *The Peoples of Philadelphia: A History of Ethnic Groups and Lower Class Life, 1790-1940* (Philadelphia: Temple University Press, 1973).

[3] Neil Harris has dealt knowingly with the phenomenon of confidence in Victorian America in *Humbug: The Art of P. T. Barnum* (Boston: Little, Brown and Company, 1973), 205-231, 279-292.

[4] Conwell, "Home Next to Church," 4-5. See A Note on Sources and the Development of an Interpretation, 180-182, for a sampling of sermons taking "home" or some related matter as a homily topic. Conwell's biographies give generous coverage of the domestic life of his subjects. See particularly *Life and Public Services of Rutherford B. Hayes* (Boston: B. B. Russell and Co., 1876), 17-65, 190-200; *Life Travels and Literary Career of Bayard Taylor* (Boston: B. B. Russell and Co., 1880), 13-41; and *The Romantic Rise of a Great American (John Wanamaker)*, 1-19, 149-170.

[5] Conwell, "Home Next to Church," 5.

[6] Russell H. Conwell, "The Country Home," *Temple Review*, XXIV, No. 12 (March 23, 1916), 3, TC.

[7] *Ibid.*

[8] *Ibid.*

[9] *Ibid.*

[10] *Ibid.*, 4.

[11] *Ibid.*

[12] *Ibid.*, 5.

[13] *Ibid.*, 7.

[14] Russell H. Conwell, "Going Back Home," *Temple Review*, XXV, No. 2 (January 12, 1917), 3, TC.

[15] *Ibid.*

[16] *Ibid.*, 4.

[17] *Ibid.*, 5.

[18] *Ibid.*, 5, 16.

[19] *Ibid.*, 16

[20] Burr, *Russell H. Conwell*, 43.

[21] The best analysis of the decline of Puritan dogma which preceeded the opening up of the American experience to the social flux, economic expansion, and religious mysticism of the early nineteenth century is Perry Miller's *Errand into the Wilderness* (New York: Harper and Row, Publishers, 1964), 184-203.

[22] For an understanding of the forces shaping the cohesion of the American home from the seventeenth to the twentieth century see John Demos, *A Little Commonwealth: Family Life in Plymouth Colony* (London: Oxford University Press, 1970); Kenneth Lockridge, *A New England Town: The First Hundred Years, Dedham, Massachusetts 1636-1736* (New York: Norton, 1970); David J. Rothman, *The Discovery of the Asylum: Social Order and Disorder in the New Republic* (Boston: Little, Brown and Company, 1971); Joseph M. Hawes, *Children in Urban Society: Juvenile Delinquency in Nineteenth-Century America* (New York: Oxford University Press, 1971); and Richard Sennett, *Families Against the Cities: Middle Class Homes of Industrial Chicago, 1872-1890* (Cambridge: Harvard University Press, 1970).

[23] The only satisfactory source showing the complexity of the social involvement in the Grace Baptist Church is May Field McKean, "Organization and Activities of the Baptist Temple" (unpublished manuscript, TC, 1916).

[24] The high degree of social interaction and cooperation in north Philadelphia in the 1880's and 1890's was strikingly similar to the activities which two perceptive historians believe typified community endeavors in the American North and Northwest during frontier stages of development. See Stanley Elkins and Eric McKitrick, "A Meaning for Turner's Frontier," *Political Science Quarterly*, LXIX (September and December, 1954), 321-353, 565-602.

[25] The fact that for an uncertain but lengthy period Laura Carnell, the woman most responsible for the day-to-day operation of Temple College, lived in the Conwell household strengthens this point. See footnote 75, Chapter I.

[26] All were in their twenties or early thirties by 1900.

[27] Tuttle, *Life with Grandfather*, 17.

[28] *Ibid.*, 18.

[29] Russell H. Conwell, "Whom to Marry," *Temple Review*, XX, No. 6 (November 3, 1911), 2, TC.

[30] *Ibid.*

[31] Two notable studies of sexual anxieties in the period are Peter T. Cominos, "Late-Victorian Secual Respectability and the Social System," *International Review of Social History*, VII (1963), 18-48, 216-250 and Ben Barker-Benfield, "The Spermatic Economy: A Nineteenth Century View of Sexuality," in *The American Family in Social-Historical Perspective*, ed. by Michael Gordon (New York: St. Martin's Press, 1973, 336-372.

[32] Russell H. Conwell, "Marriage and Divorce," *Temple Review*, XII, No. 33 (May 13, 1904), 3, TC.

[33] Russell H. Conwell, "An Ideal Democracy," *Temple Review*, XXVI (November 3, 1918), 5, TC.

[34] Russell H. Conwell, "Divorce," *Temple Review*, XX, No. 7 (November 10, 1911), 2, TC.

[35] *Ibid.*, 3.

[36] The argument that Victorian values and underlying anxieties existed in a symbiotic relationship is not new. Freud's work was permeated with this assumption. See particularly Sigmund Freud, *Civilization and Its Discontents*, translated by James Strachey (New York: W. W. Norton and Company, 1962). Such an assumption pervades the aforementioned works (footnote 31) of Cominos and Barker-Benfield. The case of the functional use of anxieties is best made recently by Nathan Hale, Jr.'s excellent *Freud and the Americans: The Beginnings of Psychoanalysis in the United States* (New York: Oxford University Press, 1971), especially in his discussion of the Victorian ideology of "civilized morality," 462-480.

[37] Russell H. Conwell, "Mother's Day," *Temple Review*, XXI, No. 38 (July 24, 1913), 4.

[38] *Ibid.*, 5.

[39] *Ibid.*

[40] *Ibid.*, 6.

[41] Russell H. Conwell, "Out of the Floods" (unpublished manuscript, TC, 1898).

[42] Of course, the nature of the sermon is didactic. "Acres of Diamonds" was only the most famous of numerous lectures with a "moral" punch. *The Angel's Lily* (Philadelphia: The Judson Press, 1920); *The Jolly Earthquake or the Power of a Cheerful Spirit* (Philadelphia: The Temple Review*, 1917); and *Six Nights in the Garden of Gethsemane* (New York: Fleming H. Revell, 1924) were typical Conwellian lectures sorting "right" from "wrong." Each of his biographies had heavy didactic purpose. A typical one was *The Romantic Rise of a Great American*, i-x, 220-225.

[43] Conwell, "Out of the Floods," 194-195. The matter of "right" and "wrong" notions of womanhood may have arose in the Jackson era. See Barbara Welter, "The Cult of True Womanhood: 1820-1860," *American Quarterly*. XVIII (Summer, 1966), 151-174.

[44] *Ibid.*, 195.

[45] *Ibid.*, 27.

[46] *Ibid.*, 28-30.

[47] *Ibid.*, 268.

[48] *Ibid.*, 32-33.

[49] *Ibid.*, 34-35.

[50] The "home" as a traditional middle class bulwark against the confusions and uncertainties of American life has been commented upon astutely by a historian and a sociologist. See John Demos, *A Little Commonwealth: Family Life in Plymouth Colony*, 180-190 and Richard Sennett, *Families Against the Cities: Middle Class Homes in Industrial Chicago*. Not all contemporary writers lauded the home as a refuge. Most conspicuous was Charlotte Perkins Gilman, particularly her *The Home, Its Work and Influence* (New York: Charlton Company, 1903). Mrs. Gilman attacked the insulation of home and its crippling effect on human potential. Conwell would have disagreed vehemently with her assessment of the American middle class home as a place which "checks the growth of love," 167. Her attack on the sequestered home only showed the reality of what she despised. For an assessment of Gilman see Carl N. Degler, "Charlotte Perkins Gilman on the Theory and Practice of Feminism," *American Quarterly*, VIII (Spring, 1956), 21-39.

[51] Russell H. Conwell, "Definition of Selfishness," *Temple Review*, XVII (June 13, 1909), 3-4, TC.

[52] Russell H. Conwell, "Fighting a Dream," *Temple Review*, XI, No. 33 (May 15, 1903), 5, TC.

[53] Conwell, *The Angel's Lily*, 16. (Published in 1920 when Conwell was almost eighty.)

[54] Russell H. Conwell, "Religion and Business," *The Temple Magazine*, V, No. 11 (March 16, 1893), 122-123.

[55] An illuminating discussion of the effect of "distended" business methods on small town America is found in Robert Wiebe, *The Search for Order, 1877-1920*, 11-43.

[56] For examples of this consensus on Conwell's contribution to popular ideology see Merle Curti, *The Growth of American Thought* (New York: Harper and Row, Publishers, 1943), 619-620, 630-631; Ralph Henry Gabriel, *The Course of American Democratic Thought* (New York: The Ronald Press Company, 1956), 158, 166; and Phillip Wyllie, *The Self-Made Man in America* (New Brunswick, New Jersey: Rutgers University Press, 1954), 59, 62, 65, 174.

[57] The best general description of the normative stance of Victorians who were uneasy about the emergence of relativism is Walter E. Houghton's, *The Victorian Fame of Mind 1830-1870* (New Haven: Yale University Press, 1957). It is assumed Houghton's generalizations about the vulnerability of the Victorian mind to currents of modernity is cross-cultural, applying to America in the mid and late nineteenth century. An interesting attempt to show the connection between Victorian values and another popular American is William G. McLoughlin's *The Meaning of Henry Ward Beecher: An Essay on the Shifting Values of Mid-Victorian America 1840-1870* (New York: Alfred A. Knopf, 1970). This study in some respects, is modeled on McLoughlin's work, although he sees Conwell only as an unambiguous representative of materialistic individualism, 117.

[58] Russell H. Conwell, *Acres of Diamonds* (Philadelphia: Reprinted by Temple University, n.d.), 13, TC.

[59] *Ibid.*, 29.

[60] *Ibid.* 47.

THE CONWELLIAN STYLE

"In the progress of civilization, through achievements greater than the electric light or steam engine, than the marvelous revelations of modern science, I see beyond us a church standing alongside, having progressed equally with them."

—Russell H. Conwell, *The Temple Magazine*[1]

"Your delightfully womanly note enclosing the five dollars for the poor children was a special encouragement to me. So deep an impression has it made on me that several times today I have stopped and asked God to send you some particular blessing. . . . I suppose the treasurer has sent you a receipt."

—Russell H. Conwell to a Baptist Temple member.[2]

Russell Conwell's beliefs appear nostalgic. They were similar to an earlier American outlook, one steeped in backward-looking Jacksonian and mid-Victorian values.[3] It is tempting to picture him wholly as an anxious man of the past who was attempting to resolve his personal struggles with the symbols that represented a young America. To characterize Conwell as backward-looking suggests that Americans of his era were out of touch with an emerging modern world. Unfortunately, such an interpretation misleads while it illuminates.

Conwell lived in an age entangled in the growth of institutions which attended the process of modernization. In the late nineteenth and early twentieth centuries the heart of modernity was the institutionalization of economic expansion. Economic growth, of course, was not new in America. The difference in Conwell's time was one of degree and result. After the Civil War there was a more open emphasis on mammoth corporate development, on the desire for governmental intervention, and on the effect of the environment on human affairs. The result was a huge corporate overlay, a slow but steady growth of governmental functions, and an increasing tendency for thinkers to start their inquiries with questions about the social or physical environment. Although a surprisingly viable individualism countered these trends, the former's cultural strength was diminishing in the face of these powerful challenges. Conwell's America was not simply a romantic trip back to rural western Massachusetts any more than the broader meaning of America was a universal longing for an agrarian past. Americans partook of their age with fervor; most accepted if they did not eagerly embrace urban-industrialism. Hundreds of thousands left their farms for the city. And they clamored for the unparalleled educational opportunities needed to implement their dreams of mobility. If people had fears, they did not always dwell on them, much less vent them in revolutionary violence, or in socially disintegrating ventures. In short, many welcomed modernity and identified it with a progressive American future.

Since Conwell was sensitive to popular attitudes one would expect him to applaud urban-industrial development. He did. An ebullient, optimistic, and even futuristic side of Conwellian thinking countered his uneasy nostalgia. A man with an older ideology, one in some respects distrustful of the new organizations to flourish. Nowhere was the modern side of Russell Conwell more deceptive than on issues of public morality. Nonetheless, it was here that an important key to his modernity was found. Within Victorian propriety, as Conwell presented it, lay, if not moral relativism, a surprisingly tolerant institutional approach to city temptations.

In 1917 some Philadelphians were expressing their uneasiness over the impact of silent movies on public morality. Conwell voiced their concern:

> When one goes to the moving pictures—and I think we must confess that we have all been there—we have seen a great many pictures which have taught good; we have seen them exhibit

the wonders of science and beauties of nature, and we have made up our minds that somehow the profession ought to be cleansed—something ought to be done, and it is strange that we who have been preaching for fifty years have not hit upon the remedy for the evil. But we have been extremists; we have said, "keep away altogether from the theater; there may be some good in it, but there is so much bad in it, the safest thing is to leave it alone altogether. . . ." That has been the weak attitude of the church . . . yet our common sense has taught us plainly that there are theatrical exhibitions which elevate and teach great truths.[4]

Cleverly, Conwell tried to dispel the congregation's ambivalence over the value of movies. He unearthed a historical church which sanctioned the use of the theater. Parishioners were reminded that "originally the theater itself was the product of the church, and used for the purpose of teaching Christians doctrines in the church long before it was ever taken over by the world."[5] While quieting their apprehension Conwell had justified an institutional solution to the problem of movies versus the prevailing morality. If the historical church approved of some kinds of public entertainment Conwell intimated that a modern church could do the same. He still, however, needed to explain to practically-minded Philadelphians how a church could be substituted for conscience as the arbiter of public morality. The pastor was equal to the task, if not entirely convincing.

The Catholic church, Conwell pointed out, was a contemporary institution which had solved the problem of individual moral confusion over the merit of movies. That he could use the Catholic church revealed both the depth of the congregation's concern and their confidence in Conwell. Throughout American history the Catholic church was depicted as one of the most insidious enemies of individual freedom. It ranked with slavery as a symbol of corruption, a veritable anti-Christ.[6] Certainly Protestant institutions had traditionally been watchful of its presence. Yet as the nineteenth century closed, Americans were participating in a self-conscious quest for consensus, unity, and community. And where could one find a better example of solidarity than within the institutional operations of the Catholic church? Their "white list" of movies and plays which were morally acceptable was worth considering.[7] New urban art forms threatened remembered domestic values and hence called for extraordinary action. Conwell asked the Temple congregation to "join with the Catholic church in purifying the theater until it is safe for your children or mine, or your friends and mine to attend."[8] Institutional control was being substituted for individual judgment. It was a minor but typical commutation of the age.

Conwell's position on public morality remained consistent during the Philadelphia years. He never unequivocally condemned such diversions as dancing, the theater, and gambling. Always the solution was not the total elimination of amusements, but *how to control them* for Christian purposes. In 1890 he saw the issue of morality in America's Victorian cities as a battle for Christian sensibilities, a struggle which had raged since Biblical times.[9] Even though the church for centuries had been victorious over the forces of Satan, modern America was slipping back into the devil's camp. The breathren were told that "the church has retreated in such confusion from so much of its former territory . . . that all is confusion and alarm in every border." Once music, song, dance, and theater were in the province of the church and worked for the cause of Christ but now they seemed "altogether in the power of evil."[10] Even "the noble game of baseball" had "become the tool of Sabbath breaking gamblers and has become so closely associated with immoral crowds which gather to bet on the results, as to be a mighty engine of evil."[11] Conwell did not lead his congregation to despair; a modern America could still be good. He urged the audience to "gather into troops, devise plans and execute them O ye people of God." Philadelphians were urged to avoid "extreme doctrines of separation of Church and State" and to be "open in the expression of religious convictions in connection with political matters."[12] Somehow the house of Christianity had to reclaim "amusements."

The problem of public morality did not abate in the twentieth century. Conwell refused to damn modern diversions and continued to try to sequester them for good purposes. To the Methodist insistence that the Bible condemned card playing Conwell replied, "the scriptures do not expressly teach that you shall not play cards." Likewise the scriptures did not "teach that dancing itself is wrong," but only wrongly used.[13] Conwell gave a clear statement where he felt the Temple should stand on modernity versus morals. There would be no tribal-like intolerant fundamentalism, characteristic of small town agrarian-minded America, within a church in a city of over one million people:

> I cannot say that the Church is against any innocent forms of theatrical amusement. It is against their association with evil, and it is against their use for a bad purpose. We are not against mankind. We love mankind; yet many of them are wicked. We must be against their wickedness, but not against them. We want to save the sinner, but we hate his sin. So we would love to save to the world every innocent game, every innocent sport, every exhibition upon the stage that is pure and teaches good morals, uprightness and religion. We would like to save them but we hate their sin and their association with sin.[14]

Amusements in Philadelphia were instrumental; they could be used for good or evil. Conwell recognized the need for a variety of social activities in a modern city. He implied that institutional control of fun would insure correct behavior. John Dewey and other progressives talked about the instrumentality of social phenomena the way Conwell did of public diversion.[15]

At the high tide of the Progressive era in 1912 Conwell gave his most complete view of entertainment in urban America. It emphasized a lofty biological basis for the necessity of community amusement. Natural urges and God's plan made "social life . . . a necessity for human development in its best form." There was no mistaking that "a desire to be with one's own fellow kind is an original appetite of the human soul" which man's Maker had installed.[16] The elemental aspects of human welfare were best satisfied through Christian entertainments, not *ad hoc* street recreation that invariably degenerated. Philadelphia lacked wholesome outlets for the social energies of its young and thus encouraged the multiplication of urban vice. The City of Brotherly Love was hardly that because of neglect of the proper forms of public morality. What was needed was "a place where the young people can safely go, and where the moral and religious people of the city will go; a place under the protection of moral associations where they can be cared for and the necessity of their nature provided for." In other words, the natural urges of young Philadelphians should be socially channeled into marriage, for of "all the appetites of life, the appetite for marriage" was the most apt to become "degraded to the saloon."[17] The irregular entertainments of the city such as second-rate movies and theater, the gaming den, the saloon, poolroom, and the dance hall threatened the social basis of the Christian home. Ideal domiciles and their intimate identities were now competing with a variety of urban temptations.

Conwell's answer to urban immorality was not to retreat into nostalgia. He responded to the moral crisis like a social worker: "Instead of striving by law, by imprisonment, by cruelty toward those who have been driven to sin, we ought in care and kindness to reach out our hands and hearts to help them to better things. . . ."[18] He proposed that the city of Philadelphia should purchase a theater (he suggested the Philadelphia Opera House), and provide the kinds of entertainments which would "elevate" the young. Successful public theater endeavors, he noted, had been proven in Germany, England, and even in Northhampton, Massachusetts. Like many progressives he suggested that all denominations in Philadelphia "who love humanity" would cooperate with the city in establishing a Christian theater to "keep our young people from the streets, from the saloons, from the slums, and furnish them with drawing entertainment." Conwell finished the plea for the progress of social morality in the spirit of twentieth century boosterism; he implored that "for heaven's sake and for humanity's sake do not let Philadelphia be behind in everything."[19]

Few doubted that Conwell wanted the young to adhere to the prevailing Victorian code of "civilized morality."[20] Nothing in the regimen for students and faculty members at the Temple College hinted at anything but the highest ethical standards.[21] Still, Conwell's public statements showed he allowed a degree of social interaction which hardly tried to duplicate the moral demands of small town America. The stress was on the institutional control of morality, and, although he never denied individuals should make moral decisions, he felt the *setting* often determined the fate of character. Much of his life was spent in creating the *proper* urban institutional environment. When after the mid-1890's Conwell found organizational innovation more difficult and self-satisfaction more remote, it did not alter a significant reality: Russell Conwell lived in one of the world's ten largest cities for over fifty years.[22] As an urban leader of America's largest Protestant church and the president of a pioneering college for the lower-middle classes, he was an institutional creature. He inhabited the domain of modern organizations most of his life. Like any successful twentieth century businessman he knew the value of flexibility and hence avoided extremes whenever possible. Conwell never tired of pointing out the virtues of the middle road and the joys of equilibrium.[23] Little wonder he was a leading sage for the American *middle* class. And so it was with his stand on public morality. There was nothing in Conwell's social outlook or even inner struggle driving him to permanently abandon the city for the loneliness of Walden pond. Philadelphia might be an evil place but it was susceptible to good. He never publicly lost hope for a Christian world in a modern setting.[24]

It was as the leader of an institutional complex trying to improve the character of an emerging urban-industrial world that the configuration of Conwell's modernity was shaped. Here the psychic crisis, originating in an earlier historical environment, merged into institutional realities and a special personal style. The coming of giant corporations was not the only agglomeration of the age; something more than external structures and functions were being contoured to the demands of a new America.

Conwell's style in Philadelphia not only suggested the outlines of institutional leadership in an era of massive transition, but also allowed a further insight into his inner crisis. By implication the crisis of American individualism becomes clearer. One cause of personal crisis in Conwell's time was the problem of Americans adjusting to the new institutional setting. Ponderous structures which directed human effort toward production were increasingly dictating roles. Whether it was a factory, a church, a school, or a hospital, sheer size coupled with efficiency techniques usually meant a loss of individual control of roles. Role transformation meant crisis for American individualism. In many ways an antebellum man, Conwell found himself directing modern institutions. Conwellian style would be, in part, a tension between pre-war conceptions and the new institutional milieu.[25] His role in the Temple complex was a window into a larger cultural crisis. Conwell's institutional style duplicated the way middle class Americans felt the transition to modernity should be made, if it should be made at all. The exchange of confidences between pastor and congregation involved a commutation of the first magnitude. Conwell was showing the way American individualism could survive the role-mutations of modernization.

There was a distinct operational dimension to Conwell's administrative style, a work-a-day world image which was carefully cultivated. A curious blend of personal flamboyance was combined with impersonal efficiency. The contrast between an open exaggerated individualism and a closed faceless organization was apparent in his *modus operandi*. Put differently, Conwell displayed two sorts of operational behavior. One was a public image which exuded warmth and intimacy. Dispensing homeness became the trademark of his ministerial style. Temple College was a home-away-from-home where the young received moral and practical direction from a watchful institutional parent. Another was his working methodology. Considerations of speed and system directed responses to all the functional requirements. This did not mean that efficiency became essential only in areas of finance. Organizational technique was crucial to the success of Conwell's entire institutional style. The inner feelings of his followers, as well as the functional demands of large scale institutions, depended on it.

The spontaneity and warmth of the weekly Baptist Temple Sunday services were calculated, not accidental. In the 1880's a visiting Methodist minister attended a typical church service. His comments illustrated the planned intimacy which colored Conwell's ministerial approach. The visitor marveled at "the unusual spirit of homeness about the place" which he had never experienced in a church. It was remarkable and disarming the way "everybody moved about and greeted each other with an ease" he felt was all too rare in American churches. The atmosphere was almost too relaxing: "some people [abused] the liberty of the place by whispering, even during the sermon."[26] When a lady offered him a hymn book he was startled, but Conwell's selection of old-fashioned hymns was reassuring. When it came time for the collection:

> It was not asking for money at all. The preacher put his notice of it the other way about. He said, "The people who wish to worship God by giving their offering into the trust of the church could place it in the baskets which would be passed to anyone who wanted to give." It was all voluntary, and really

an offering to the Lord. I had never seen such a way of doing things in a church collection. I do not know if the minister of the church *required it so.*[27]

The observer concluded that, "The whole service was as simple as simple can be—and it was surely as sincere as simple." And yet, he seemed aware of the necessity for some system of simplicity ("I do not know if the minister or church required it so.")[28]

An unpublished survey of the Baptist Temple's operational policies removes any question of whether there was method in Conwell's institutional style. In 1916 a church secretary, May Field McKean, wrote about Conwellian procedures in two tracts entitled "Organization and Activities of the Baptist Temple" and "The Book of Methods for the Baptist Temple."[29] McKean revealed the basis for the church's institutional operation:

> Mr. Conwell believes that the business principles which apply to a banking house should apply also to a church. Therefore when the Temple was built a full set of offices was provided, with every convenience and appliance that would be found in the most modern business house.[30]

The extension of "business principles" into church affairs was far from modest. Each new church member's name was automatically transferred to an efficient accounting system. When a new name was entered on the church roll it was also entered into the business records. This was done so that the new member could "assume a future share, according to ability, of the support of the church." The accounting system was directly related to the intimacy one felt when the Temple congregation gathered each Sunday morning. The "sittings in the Temple" were assigned to all "regular givers" regardless of whether or not they were church members so "that they may be made to feel as much 'at home' in the church service as they would at their own table where each member of the family has his own particular place."[31] Something as crucial as the feeling of homeness in a Conwellian institution could not be left to chance.

Circumstance made Conwell more conscious of the need to regulate church finances with greater predictability. Once the deacons by 1895 had curtailed his ability to create new institutions through proselyizing for "fairs, concerts, lecture courses, dinners, and various other forms of entertainments" it was logical to seek a safer kind of financing.[32] The practice of "systematic giving" through "duplex envelopes," which the deacons encouraged, was not out of place to a pastor who equipped the Baptist Temple like a modern office.[33] A man who systematized prayer would not resist the facelessness of "systematic giving." In 1916, cards displaying the following message were handed to every person attending the Sunday service:

> *Dear Friend:*
>
> *I wish that you would take this card home and write to me why you wish us to pray for you. It gives me an added interest and directness and it will avoid the danger of forgetting. When your prayer is answered I would like to hear about it.*
> *But all communication will be kept to myself.*
>
>

Your brother,

Russell H. Conwell[34]

The magnitude and explicitness of Conwell's organization capacity showed up in a multitude of other church activities. There were established procedures for greeting guests. A committee was formed to process strangers into the ways of Templana. The group greeted newcomers, introduced them to the pastor and other church officials, gave them a thorough tour of the building, and otherwise acted "as a general 'information bureau',"[35] A unique system of providing for regular choir attendance while simultaneously collecting a small revenue was established. Any person not attending the practice session was required to pay twenty-five cents for each absence.[36]

There was a wide variety of working organizations which Conwell either started or endorsed. Among them was a Bible School which McKean called a "department of the 'church at study'." A Christian Endeavor Society was divided into "sections" representing affiliated ages and interests. The children's church was a kind of religious kindergarten, formed so children could be "led to Christ."A number of charity service clubs, such as the Brotherhood Mission, the Ladies Missionary Circle, the Ladies Aid Society, the Samaritan Aid, and the Garretson Aid, dispensed sympathy and service to the sick and poor of north Philadelphia. The Beneficial Association, for men and women, was a church insurance company which McKean proudly reported operated "upon a wholly Christian business basis," providing cash benefits for infirmity or death. Persons of the proper moral character were encouraged to join, and any surplus cash was applied to the next year's dues. The Baptist Temple Men's Class grew out of the Conwell Men's Class (a Sunday School for adult males) and functioned as a forum to discuss contemporary problems of Victorian manhood. Conwell organized the Temple Guard, a para-military organization for adolescent boys which encouraged discipline in young men at an age when McKean thought "it is sometimes difficult to hold them in the church." Completing the principal church organizations were two choirs, the chorus and the Temple Glee Club for men.[37]

This abundance of church-related groups was responsible to Conwell and the deacons. Nevertheless, there were an extraordinary number of church officers involved in the various organizations. This hierarchical complexity made the church seem office-like. The officers of the Temple Sunday School included: General Superintendent, Assistant Superintendent, Superintendent Primary Department, General Secretary, Secretary Senior Department, Assistant Secretary Junior Department, Secretary Primary Department, Treasurer, Financial Secretary, Registrar, Secretary of Supplies, Secretary of Teachers, Librarian, Statistician, and Chorister.[38] By the second decade of the twentieth century the administrative structure of Grace Baptist Church resembled that of a large corporation. Somehow Conwell's carefully nurtured home-like atmosphere of the Baptist Temple thrived in a labyrinth of bureaucratic procedures and structure.

If Conwell ran a thoroughly modern church, he also encouraged the development of modern business procedures in Temple College. In the early 1890's he wrote to the secretary of the college trustees, Charles Stone, about the need for an administrative bureaucracy. Conwell was concerned about the lack of order and decision-making power in the school's administration. He told Stone that the college's faculty must learn that Temple was a "school not a mob," and be governed as such.[39] Conwell equated the modernization of the school's administration with the latest business techniques. Stone was informed in 1893 about the inadequacy of a Miss Dellow who was then auditing the college accounts. Although the woman was "scrupulously honest" she did not know anything of "systematic bookkeeping." Miss Dellow had concocted her own bookkeeping scheme and Conwell found it futile to "compare vouchers or study out the intricacies of a system" only she understood. In the future the accounts were to be made in a "systematic thorough manner" so the deacons could accurately interpret the church's business.[40]

Much of Conwell's desire to modernize the college's business procedures sprung from concern for the school's survival. In the early nineties he was most anxious about how the college would pay back the church after buying part of its property. The transaction involved some complicated financial maneuvering. Without systematic bookkeeping and a college finance manager who was a "thorough going businessman" the financial status of the college could not be stabilized.[41] If the college was lost, Conwell's credibility would be shattered. An internal ordering of the college finances would not only solidify institutional walls but fortify the pastor's reputation as a successful innovator. But for Conwell the problem was more complicated. Unless the college survived he could not success-fully control his old inner crisis. The lingering self-reproach now being displaced into the construction of institutions would not be satisfied if the creations went under. Conwell had claimed going into armed battle to resolve the Johnny Ring affair; surely he would not hesitate about using modern "overreaching" methods to save the college. If the latest accounting system was impersonal and contradicted the nostalgia of a remembered past, it had the virtue of accommodating current personal difficulties. But the respite was only momentary. These same bureaucratic tendencies worked to limit Conwell's freedom to innovate, and, as intimated, eventually helped bring his nervous collapse. He found that what relieved also led to a more un-resolvable situation. To retain the link with his origins, to insure a proper channeling of old anxieties, Conwell initiated procedures at the Temple institutions making the realization of his inner needs more tenuous. Yet, its very remoteness made the world of South Worthington and the memory of Johnny Ring more desirable. In the life of Russell Conwell (and perhaps in the life of his America) modernity strengthened the call of nostalgia, while undermining its reality.

One historian has maintained that much can be learned about popular attitudes through examining the testimonials to businessmen at their deaths.[42] A look at Conwellian memorabilia might give clues about what in his style engaged the popular imagination. The testimonials were often local, leading to a suspicion that Conwell's institutional endeavors formed an important part of his fascination. When the eulogies were combined with praises for an aging but famous Conwell a significant theme emerged: at the end of his life he was characterized as a symbolic father. The image of an institutional sire as well as the magic of "Acres of Diamonds" occupied the attention of admirers at the end.

In death he was compared with Abraham Lincoln. Conwell would have liked the similitude.[43] Both had administered home-spun wisdom from a position of institutional power. As young men with rural beginnings, they lost a beloved lady, and practiced law. Duty called each to the throne of responsibility; neither was happy there, but both accepted the call. There was a vast difference between the burden of the Presidency and a few Philadelphian institutions, still the analogy was not far-fetched. The death of both evoked images of losing a father.[44]

Conwell was revered as the man "back of" the church, university, and hospital. He had shown Philadelphians that there was nothing anemic in modern Christianity. Conwell had been "the most virile and aggressive and manly personality" who had ever worked "for the uplift of Philadelphia." Here lay "the silent body" of one of the most productive institution builders of the times, a Victorian father who wasted not a whit of his God-given masculinity.[45]

There were other images of a fatherly Conwell. In 1893, as a tribute to his fiftieth birthday, the Baptist Temple's secretary, May Field McKean, composed a poem paying homage to her employer's paternal qualities. "The Flight of the Eagle" put to verse not a man rooted in institutional life, but a free cruising spirit.[46] Here was a boundless Jacksonian adventurer who took "his perservering, unassisted, way to dizzy heights." Conwell, in McKean's eyes, was not an institutional father who accepted the confinements of modern life. Rather he, like the eagle, soared in the upper air of freedom, "till the haunts of men far, far below" seemed like "a prison cell."[47] Before the deacons curtailed his

91

creativity Conwell was colored more the bold fanciful bachelor, than a dutiful father. Temple's pastor was envied for his ability to live in a fading American past.

Still McKean made sure her Conwell did not stray too far from the "Eagle's Nest." Conwell was never "The Eagle" but always "Our Eagle." The paternal overtones were illustrated on the poem's final page which simply pictured an eagle feeding its young in a lofty nest. There was an obvious contradiction between a "pastor, shepherding the flock with tenderest care" and a free spirit seeking escape from "the haunts of men."[48] As father he attracted with both centripetal and centrifugal force. Nonetheless, the dominant symbolism of "The Flight of the Eagle" was a God-like, free-wheeling individual endowed with powers beyond those of ordinary people, a being who escaped entrapment in contemporary institutions. The free father wandered away from modernity and never really left home. McKean poetized Conwell's inner struggle and hinted at the strains of an American transition. Was what sparked her imagination the vision of a Conwell who appeared to have transcended present perplexities? Anyone that capable must be close to the heavenly father, the same who gave Conwell "the wings and power and strength to fly above the earth to the vaulted sky."[49] Only gods transcended history; the implication was obvious.

The first half of Conwell's life was lived in drift. Not until past forty did he settle into his final occupation, and settling down in the City of Brotherly Love was partially illusory. The lecture circuit and many trips to his retreat, the Eagle's Nest in South Worthington, kept him away for substantial periods. But the need for an institutional life remained. Images of a virile creator and an Emersonian Eagle did not exhaust his paternal repertoire.

An aged woman characterized Conwell as a salutary combination of love and authority; a kind of benevolent dictator who gave security and moral direction simultaneously. Letters from an Ellen (Nellie) Frances Mills to Conwell when he was in his seventies showed another kind of father—one more comfortable in an institutional role. Nellie's correspondence was inflated, gushy, sentimental poetry commemorating her idol's birthdays. The poems were filled with child-like deference to a strong but loving father, one who was a pillar of moral strength in a troubled world. Conwell's reputation was secure because, "Every day from sun to sun/Countless millions bless your name." With Victorian urgency Conwell was told that the world needed him *"more* and *more, Need* your *counsel o'er* and *o'er.*"[50] Three years before his death Nellie fully developed Conwell into a paternalistic institutional father. The verse was pure corn but the content showed charismatic authority coming from a different source than "The Flight of the Eagle":

> Hospitals and schools to meet a need
> A church far greater than a creed
> Few men there are in any land
> Hath reared a monument so grand
> With little thought of self in mind
> But for the good of all mankind.[51]

Here was a man who embraced socially serving institutions as accomplished facts. Nellie Mills spoke more than she knew and saluted Conwell as a "Veteran soldier of the Cross/Who counts no sacrifice a loss."[52] She touched upon both the transition to an America of institutions and the springs of a psychic crisis inherent in the metamorphosis.

Those who praised Conwell in life and death, then, saw him as several kinds of fathers. To a few acquaintances at death he was a builder—a creator of manly, uplifting institutions. A church secretary described him as a limitless free spirit, but one who remained attached to community. And, to an aged female admirer, he was the rock of institutional strength in the quicksands of modern America. Although each of these visions was special they converged on one common particular; all deferred in Conwell's authority. It was not simply an acquiescence to power; the reverse was more the case. He deserved their respect because he typified and removed the ambivalence of American power wrapped in idealism. An era which often distrusted modern people and organizations cherished the symbol of a fatherly Russell Conwell who reassured them that America could have substantial institutional power and yet be good. Testimonials on Conwell's role in Philadelphia came to substantially the same conclusions as the thousands who applauded "Acres of Diamonds"; there need not be unease about modern forms when such a man as Russell Conwell and his creations bespoke of a successful transition. Individualism and social endeavor, idealism and materialism, remembered homes and the modern establishment worked for each other. They had enough confidence in a paternal Conwell to make him the symbol of the consummate American merger, the amalgamation of appearance and reality. Conwell's individualism was unflinchingly corporate. Here was a man whose life effectively blurred the strains between past and present in a age of momentous transition.

What then can be said of Conwell's institutional style? From the days of recruiting for the Union Army in the Berkshires his organization talent lay in building from the ground up. During the late 1860's in Minnesota Conwell created a newspaper which encouraged community uplift and was the literary blueprint of later more massive endeavors. In the 1870's he agreed to reorganize the finances of the Lexington Baptist Church and began operating as a preacher-innovator. When the Philadelphia deacons offered him greater opportunity to apply this technique there was no hesitation about leaving Massachusetts. Inexorably Conwell's inner restlessness complimented the era's need for institutional 1900 Conwell, much to his discomfort, was forced to abandon the role of institution-maker and become, more and more, the preacher-administrator. Although Conwell continued to appear as a free-wheeling creator, the new constrictions made his style seem superfluous. The result was nervous collapse and great unhappiness until the end of his life. Transformation from one role to another, though incompletly accomplished in Conwell, symbolized the larger transition from one America to another. Innovational energy was being dammed up in consolidation. The drying up of opportunities for Conwell's open-ended institutional style microscopically reflected a profound metamorphosis in American life. This national transition has been commented upon frequently, but Conwell's *modus operandi* in Philadelphia reveals more than a collaboration.

There was subtlety in Conwell's duplication of the larger process. His style illuminated the middle class response to the stresses of being transmuted from one era to another. He was able to convince them that there was nothing undemocratic, anti-individualistic, or impersonal about bureaucratic institutions. Sociologists Alexis de Tocqueville and Max Weber, historian Robert Wiebe, and psychologist Sigmund Freud are helpful from a theoretical perspective in seeing Conwell ease this transition. Since the transition was corporate in the fullest sense—meaning sociological and psychological as well as historical—it is fitting to use a corporate, i.e., interdisciplinary approach to help evaluate the impact of Conwellian style.

If in any democracy there were always tensions between individualism and conformity, as Tocqueville assumed, it was logical that some historical eras would hold extremes of one or both tendencies.[53] Robert Wiebe has argued that there was indeed an ultra-individualism in America during the late nineteenth century. The populist uprisings of the 1890's were, in many ways, extensions of the dominant individualistic anti-corporation campaigns of the Jacksonians. They were reactions to an increasingly corporate and therefore institutional America, an America whose work-a-day world demanded increasing conformity and standardization. The strikes and other popular disorders of this period, as well as those in the young twentieth century, were instructive; they revealed both the magnitude of change and the internal strain which followed the swing of the democratic pendulum from individual to institutional dominance.[54] But why did the new organizations become bureaucratic? Weber is the most helpful. He expanded Tocqueville's idea about the necessity of conformity in a democratic society. Weber believed mass democracy always produced bureaucratic organizations. As long as democratic units remained small and homogeneous the phenomenon of bureaucracy did not arise.[55] If this is correct, it is futile to look for the origins of American institutional bureaucracy in the late nineteenth or early twentiety century. One would do better to examine the first half of the nineteenth century for the beginnings of this development. Indeed, in Weber's context the whole of America's democratic experience might be interpreted as a germation and growth of the bureaucratic process. Any discussion of a crisis in American individualism would involve not only its relationship with conformity and institutions, but with a *particular stage* of bureaucratic development. Conwell's contribution was to create the *illusion* of balance between individualism, innovative institutionalism, and a particular stage of bureaucratic growth. He was able to contain his own anxieties (with the exception of his breakdown) and those of Temple parishioners through presenting a style of institution-alism which pretended not to be institutional at all—if institutional meant the abridgment of individual choice and a remembered personalized past. It has been recently observed that modern leadership *must* personalize itself.[56] Modern institutions tend to dissipate responsibility; the masses of people lose the loci of authority which existed in more traditional societies. The result is loneliness and loss of direction. All institutionalized citizens grope for legitimate authority and responsibility which, because of bureaucratic depersonalization, none can have. Charismatic leadership becomes a substitute for the poverty of personal authority and responsibility in modern institutions. Leadership becomes a substitute for the shortcoming of organization.[57]

The Temple institutions were emerging as fully-developed modern bureaucracies. The growing complexity of their authority structures indicated that personal responsibility was indeed being dissipated. Moreover, the fast growing urban environment of north Philadelphia was a part of a volatile mass democracy. The social needs of this mushrooming area were immense and institutional responses had to be proportionately gigantic. Conwell not only bent with this urbanizing tide, he was a little ripple who helped make it. A cultivated image as a charismatic paternal figure, who was free of, and yet responsible for, his community, was appropriate in a developing bureaucratic complex. It gave him the authority to help reduce the strains and confusions of urban life in north Philadelphia. Conwell urged those living in the area to be a part of the Baptist Temple, to become members of its related organizations. They could, he continually said, have a place and a sense of belonging in a city lacking remembered security. This was a man who appeared to have everything they wanted: the values of the past, the hopes for the future, and the power to implement them. To participate in Grace Church or enroll in Temple College was less perplexing because of the charismatic appeal of Conwell's reputation and style, conveniently combined in the same image. Take away Conwell and the link with the past was lost, and the hope for the future flimsy. Without "The Flight of the Eagle" thousands of Philadelphians could not have flown from the nineteenth to the twentiety century so painlessly.

Hence, Conwell's institutional style eased the transition from an individualistic to an institutional democracy. A life in Philadelphia and "Acres of Diamonds" showed how the crisis in

American individualism could be resolved. When he had the nerve to tell his brethren that the Catholic Church had found a suitable institutional solution to the touchy issue of movies, Conwell exhibited the convincing capacity of Conwellian style. After all, their pastor had built the largest Protestant church in America and yet had preserved nostalgia within its modern walls. Did not his life testify to the outstanding success an individual could have in an institutional setting? Since Conwell had correctly interpreted the relationship between the individual and the church since the 1880's, why have doubts now?

Acceptance of the Conwellian style pointed toward another dimension of his functional capacity. A description of Conwell's charisma does not adequately illuminate the outlines of transition. Russell Conwell did more than ease transitional anxieties. His style pointed toward a more gripping psychological encounter, one which at first seems less sensitive to historical timing.

Throughout the sermons and lectures and in the purposes of the Temple complex runs a familiar and consistent refrain. Man was created by God in God's image with a highly developed sense of right and wrong. Man was more than a beast because he expressed higher purposes. Unless Conwell's utterances were pure gush and Temple institutions only a group of urban buildings—which on one level was true—the heavy moralism pervading the rhetoric and institutions was a significant part of his style. Freud's theory of guilt helps show why this style was so dependent on matters of conscience.[58] Oft-repeated doctinres of moral virtue and the creation of ethically uplifting institutions were, in the Freudian perception, evidences of deep entanglement in guilt. Modern societies were societies which had developed strong super-egos or consciences. A ubiquitous feeling of guilt in a culture indicated a society saturated with constant admonitions to do right. Highly developed cultures generated built-in moral scruples to check the aggressive drives of the human ego. The ego's cultural aggressiveness, springing from the libido or id, had from primal times denied fulfillment through the development of the super-ego. The moral demands of the conscience continually punished the ego and in the process made possible the religious restraint inherent in all civilization. Indeed, the development of civilization was dependent upon the conscience to sublimate drives. Without guilt and its attending moral structures of stable families the ever increasing incorporations of human beings into tribes, confederations, and nations was doomed. In order to bring about an international Christian brotherhood, in order to "make the world safe for democracy," a national super-ego needed nurturing. Freud implied American progressive creeds could not exist without guilt: neither could any other morality.[59]

In this setting the meaning of Conwell's life changes. His style becomes less unique, than typical. He now appears as only a vocal member of a common humanity who illustrated a pervasive psychic structure and dynamic. From this vantage point there would seem to be little functional difference between the inner predicaments of Conwell and Jesus Christ. Modernity becomes a historically elongated problem which makes the close observations of historians less satisfying. Certainly the life of Russell Conwell becomes so representative that it loses utility in helping to define an era of American transition—an age, from Freud's perspective, which extended back into the ill-defined morass of man's pre-history. Conwell's tendency to avoid extremes and blur the past with the present has a ready interpretation: In everyone's psyche compromises are made. Accommodations between the demands of the ego and admonitions of the super-ego allow people to survive. Insofar as Conwell expressed mergers between what man wanted to do and what he thought was right his style was a strong expression of common inner compromises. Hence, the problem of the morality of movies appears less a conscious Conwellian adaptation to the urban needs of Philadelphians than typical psychological adjustment.

Yet it may be that through the lens of history a common human condition becomes at certain moments painfully uncommon. During some eras of historical transition the pressures of moral conscience on the aggressive proclivities of the ego could become uncommonly intense. The battlelines within the psychic apparatus between the Civil War and World War I in America were sharply drawn. If aggressively sought change was accelerating the demands for morality, the role of guilt would be proportionately enlarged. Without jeremiad-like cries for self-sacrifice and all the attending trappings of guilt—

the longing for lost community, home, mother and father—there would not be much *psychological* evidence of a most assertive national ego during the Victorian era. Conwell's style, reputation, language, and institutions were the obverse side of a hyperactive aggressive historical moment. Just as his life and its complementing structures showed the release of powerful egotistical energies, so, too, did his obsession with morality show the underlying operation of super-ego. This dynamic contradiction, which Conwell spent his life trying to resolve, may have been writ large in his America.

In the twilight of his life and two decades into the twentieth century, a self-perpetuating bureaucracy made this drama between ego and super-ego, between inner drives fostering impersonal institutional growth and a guilty conscience, seem somewhat irrelevant. The meaning of Conwell's life and the lives of millions of Americans immersed in an agonizing historical transition had been cast as a frenetic struggle between evil forces and moral intentions. But the relativism of the second quarter of the twentieth century, one form of emerging modernity, threatened to undo the innards of Victorian style. Conwell, even though his activities after 1895 belied it, continued to expound the message of transition. Although he accommodated, soothed, and slipped into a relativism of his own, he still reverberated the passing chords of an earlier national transition. He spoke to Americans as if the battle still raged. Little wonder the style attracted with less force in an age acculturated as urban-industrial than one which was passing to city and factory. Modernity did not *need* the psychic battles of a Russell Conwell.

The one American social phenomenon which tokened the end of the romantic values of the nineteenth century more than any other was the city. It seemed to thrive in an amoral and bureaucratic milieu. Before death Conwell spoke frequently of urban matters which threatened the role of morality and hence Conwellian style as a force in American history. These were the sad laments of a man who symbolized that much more than he was dying by World War I. One kind of crisis in American individualism was being exchanged for another.

References

[1] Russell H. Conwell, *The Temple Magazine*, IV (July 1, 1892), 7, TC.

[2] Russell H. Conwell to Baptist Temple member, Miss Meredith, August 11, 1899, TC.

[3] Marvin Meyers has skillfully chartered the nostalgic side of the Jacksonian Creed in *The Jacksonian Persuasion.* Also see footnote 57, Chapter II.

[4] Russell H. Conwell, "Reasonable Christianity," *Temple Review*, XXVI (January 25, 1918), 5, TC.

[5] *Ibid.*

[6] David B. Davis, "Some Themes of Countersubversion: An Analysis of Anti-Masonic, Anti-Catholic, and Anti-Mormon Literature," *Mississippi Valley Historical Review*, XLVII (September, 1960), 205-224. Davis more fully develops the impact of the symbol of Catholicism on the American mind in *The Slave Power Conspiracy and the Paranoid Style* (Baton Rouge: Louisiana State University Press, 1969), 62-86.

[7] Conwell, "Reasonable Christianity," 5.

[8] *Ibid.*

[9] Russell H. Conwell, "Church and Amusements," *The Temple Pulpit,* II, No. 12 (October 5, 1890), 3, TC.

[10] *Ibid.*, 5.

[11] *Ibid.*, 8.

[12] *Ibid.*, 8-9.

[13] Russell H. Conwell, "Amusements," *Temple Review*, X, No. 36 (June 3, 1904), 4, TC.

[14] *Ibid.*, 5.

[15] See Wiebe's discussion of the close connection between pragmatism and twentieth century modernity in *The Search for Order, 1877-1920*, 133-163. Also perceptive is Morton White's chapter "Destructive Intelligence" in *Social Thought in America: The Revolt Against Formalism* (Boston: Beacon Press, 1968), 161-179.

[16] Russell H. Conwell, "Public Amusements," *Temple Review*, XXI, No. 13 (January 30, 1913), 3, TC.

[17] *Ibid.*, 4.

[18] *Ibid.*

[19] *Ibid.*, 5.

[20] See Nathan Hale, Jr., *Freud and the Americans: The Beginnings of Psychoanalysis in the United States*, 462-480.

[21] For example, Milton F. Stauffer (see footnote 75, Chapter I) related that, "Smoking was never permitted in or around the buildings. A member of the faculty who forgot the regulation was supposed to be reported to the president's office." Interestingly, conditions changed near the end of Conwell's life for, "when one thousand World War I veterans were enrolled," the rule against smoking "was knocked into a three-cocked hat." Milton F. Stauffer (unpublished and untitled manuscript, February 10, 1943), 10, TC.

[22] Philadelphia ranked eighth in 1890 and ninth in 1920. By 1960 the city was only seventeenth among the world's largest urban agglomerations. Eric E. Lampard, "The Urbanizing World" in *The Victorian City: Images and Realities,* edited by W. J. Dyos and Michael Wolff (London: Routledge and Kegan Paul, Ltd., 1973), 9.

[23] For instance, *The Angel's Lily* was an ode to the virtues of the *middle* class as contrasted with wealth and poverty—two unwholesome American extremes. Note the implication of equilibrium in sermons like "Reasonable Christianity"; "A Christian Strike," *Temple Review,* XXIX, No. 36 (October 28, 1921), 8-9, 13-15; "Peace through War," *Temple Review,* XXIX, No. 42 (December 9, 1921), 207; and "Limits of Liberty," *Temple Review,* XXX, No. 25 (June 23, 1922), 2-6; all in TC. For an analysis of "balance" in Conwell as a way of reducing social stress see Daniel W. Bjork, "Russell H. Conwell and the Crisis of American Individualism" (unpublished Ph.D. Dissertation, University of Oklahoma, Norman, 1973), 113-121.

[24] In 1909 Conwell announced to the Temple congregation that, "God's kingdom is coming." The modernization of the world was at hand because "Merchandise of every clime is exchanged" and "money is becoming more international." Hence, "the nearer people get together the more necessary are Christian principles for their lives. . . ." Russell H. Conwell, "Blessed Lawmakers," *The Temple Pulpit* (no volume) (February 5, 1909), 15, TC.

[25] American historians have dealt skillfully with the problem of ante-bellum creeds meeting post-bellum institutionalization. Each of the following, although emphasizing different aspects of the transformation, are incisive arguments supporting the reality of this transition: George Frederickson, *The Inner Civil War: Northern Intellectuals and the Crisis of Union*; Wiebe, *The Search for Order, 1877-1920*; R. Jackson Wilson, *In Quest of Community: Social Philosophy in the United States, 1860-1920* (New York: John Wiley and Sons, Inc., 1968), and John C. Thomas, "Romantic Reform in America," *American Quarterly,* XVII, No. 4 (Winter, 1965), 656-681.

[26] Quoted in Burr, *Russell H. Conwell.* The identity of the visiting minister is unknown.

[27] *Ibid.,* 189-190.

[28] *Ibid.,* 190.

[29] May Field McKean, "Organization and Activities of the Baptist Temple" and May Field McKean, "The Book of Methods for the Baptist Temple" (unpublished manuscripts, TC, 1916).

[30] McKean, "The Book of Methods for the Baptist Temple," 33.

[31] *Ibid.*, 34-35.

[32] *Ibid.*, 38-39.

[33] *Ibid.*, 39.

[34] *Ibid.*, 89.

[35] *Ibid.*, 33.

[36] *Ibid.*

[37] McKean, "Organization and Activities of the Baptist Temple" (no pagination).

[38] *Ibid.*

[39] Russell H. Conwell to Charles F. Stone, April 19, 1893, TC.

[40] *Ibid.*, June 29, 1893, TC.

[41] *Ibid.*, January 10, 1892, TC.

[42] Sigmund Diamond, *The Reputation of the American Businessman*, (Cambridge: Harvard University Press, 1955), 1-4.

[43] Grace Baptist Church, "Memorial Services in honor of Russell H. Conwell, Founder and President of Temple University" (unpublished manuscript, TC, 1925), 13.

[44] Walt Whitman's eulogy poems *O Captain! My Captain*, *When Lilacs Last in the Dear Yard Bloome'd*, and *This Dust Was Once the Man* show Lincoln's death cast as feeling for loss of father.

[45] *Ibid.*, 14.

[46] May Field McKean, "The Flight of the Eagle" (Philadelphia: by the author, 1893).

[47] *Ibid.*, 4-6.

[48] *Ibid.*, 10.

[49] *Ibid.*, 6.

[50] Ellen Frances Mills to Russell H. Conwell, September 15, 1920, TC. Mill's italics.

[51] *Ibid.*, February 15, 1922.

[52] *Ibid.*

[53] Alexis de Tocqueville, *Democracy in America*, translated by George Lawrence (New York: Harper and Row Publishers, 1966), 227-254, 477-484.

[54] Wiebe, *The Search for Order*, 76-110, 286-302.

[55] Max Weber, *Economy and Society*, III, Translated by Ephraim Fischoff, *et al.* (New York: Bedminster Press, 1968), 983.

[56] Peter J. Larmour, "DeGaule and the New France," *The Yale Review* (Summer, 1966), 500-520.

[57] *Ibid.*, 507.

[58] Freud, *Civilization and Its Discontents*, particularly 64-92.

[59] Freud was curious about the strength of the Messianic belief in American history. See Sigmund Freud, *The Future of an Illusion*, translated by W. D. Robson-Scott (Garden City, New York: Doubleday & Company, 1969), 27, 63, 80-81.

EPILOGUE

VICTORIAN LIMITS

Bruce Barton: Isn't there a sadness in facing the sunset so much alone?

Russell Conwell: An old man is already a citizen of two worlds. No matter whether he wakes up tomorrow here or over there, he wakes up among friends. Here, or there, he is already at home.

—"Conversation Between a Young Man and an Old Man."[1]

"In his 80th year Dr. Conwell announced from the pulpit that he wanted to start a hospital to be known as the Great Heart Hospital. This he said would be the last thing he would organize. He would not let Dean Carnell nor myself have anything to do with it. He wanted to interest entirely new people who were not at work in any one of his enterprises."

—Milton F. Stauffer to Millard E. Gladfelter.[2]

Recently, on a dreary January Sunday morning, this writer attended the worship service at the Grace Baptist Temple. The bleak weather was apropos for the neighborhood. Blocks upon blocks of weary row tenements, many dilapidated or empty, frequently interrupted the "modern" high-rise development of Temple University. The old and the new were combined in an esthetically grotesque composite. Anyone still living who was familiar with this section of Philadelphia during Conwell's last years could hardly be unaware of the radical change from a white middle class neighborhood to a black lower class ghetto—pervaded with unemployment, crime, and social tensions.[3] From the middle class perspective, here was the full horror of modern urban America. Russell Conwell would not have found the Christian brotherhood he wanted for Philadelphia. It was as if the spirit of Sally Ann Thompson had infected the area with all the modern incongruities he had feared most. Fortunately, Conwell's still remains had rested for close to fifty years in a plot on the Temple campus. He did not live to see how far America had abandoned Conwellian principles. Even so, by the 1920's the "fire bell in the night" was ringing loudly.

There were brethren in the twenties who wished to move the church to more compatible surroundings. Conwell fought the move—predictively with an innovational approach. He agreed with some in his audience that Philadelphia, indeed America, needed to be saved "from the great army of criminals which are now being raised up in our city."[4] But the way to fight urban decay was not to flee to the suburbs. Long ago he had made the decision to sink or swim in Philadelphia. Not only was age making a move absurd, but it was a neglect of duty. The inner battle he had engaged in since youth did not cease with the approach of death. To leave the Baptist Temple because the surrounding neighborhood threatened to become alien was unthinkable. The ghost of Johnny Ring still could haunt. He faced the situation. True, he told the brethren in a voice weakened after eighty years of use, "Since we built the Temple, this neighborhood has filled up with other races of people—with the Jews, the Russians, and the Negroes—until we are almost an island in this great company of people who do not worship with us." The changing urban culture had brought forth the question of "whether we should not do as other churches have done and move farther out to reach our own people" who had fled to a more compatible neighborhood. There could be only one answer, and it was no different from the Conwellian stance of the 1880's. There was only one "place to secure peace and prosperity," and it was not in suburbia. The solution was "to go down into the slums of the city, within almost a stone's throw of this Church, and set up missions, and go into the homes and see that they have the Bible." Then, and only then, would the

Ten Commandments "reach down to the humblest home."[5]

His answer to social ills was typically nineteenth century. Through moral suasion and missionary zeal a way of life compatible with Victorian middle class assumptions could be preserved if not extended. The free-wheeling innovative style which brought Conwell to the pinnacle of reputation could not be forsaken. It did not matter that the deacons had long ago decided against investing large amounts of capital in social experimentation. The imperatives of personality would run their course irrespective of outer change.

Other Americans, however, could not respond to Conwellian suggestions with the force of thirty years earlier. The 1920's were attuned to an operational rather than an innovational world. Lives were centered in the maintenance of technical tasks rather than in the demands of transitional growth.[6] People still dreamed of adventure as their predecessors did, but the new generation which came to maturity in the twenties had different moral heroes. Bruce Barton was more in step with the times than was Russell Conwell. In 1921 Barton interviewed Conwell. "Conversation Between a Young Man and an Old Man" was more than another adulation of Conwell's accomplishments.[7] It captured the subtle change in moral assumptions between the centuries, between growing up in an America becoming urban and industrial, and one which had arrived. There was a fundamental divergence between a Protestant leader who in a few years would interpret Christ in a managerial role and one who saw him as a self-sacrificing missionary doing boundless good for humanity.[8]

Barton said more than he knew when he asked Conwell a question that the twentieth century America might have asked the nineteenth: "You've played all kinds of parts—soldier, traveler, newspaper man, lawyer, preacher, lecturer, university president. There aren't any new parts left for you. Honestly, Doctor Conwell, is the world still interesting when a man is seventy-eight?"[9] Of course Conwell had played his last new role in the 1890's, even though he bravely insisted the world was still filled with wonder. Different men now shaped America; men who were molded by the parameters of occupational expertise, and not nurtured in a free-wheeling game of vocational leap-frog. Barton felt as comfortable being a Christian manager as Conwell felt estranged. The former helped to efficiently arrange the existing psychological structure of American institutional Christianity; the latter transferred older attitudes to newly created institutions. To Barton, as his question implied, Conwellian style was as defunct as the dinosaur. Their inner energies were commutated to different Americas.

Up to the end Conwell tried to control the moral direction of Temple University. A year before his death he supported opening a proper bookstore. He told the store's first manager that "it would help the university very much to guide the taste and outside instruction of a large class of people," if the establishment made available only books which were "elevating [and] instructive."[10] The consistent position that new institutions should encourage morally responsible behavior was never altered. Building a higher education to inculcate young men and women with the skills a modern urban-industrial society needed was always secondary to the didactic function of schooling. The direct bridge Conwell tried to build between righteous homes and universitiy education was an attempt to incorporate the remembered values of rural Massachusetts into a burgeoning modern Philadelphia. Moral institutions were extensions of a psychic struggle enacted during momentous historical transition. Indeed, this symbiotic relationship defined an important aspect of the transformation.

Conwell's dream of paternal institutions was not to be. Missionary work among the heathen minorities of the streets of Philadelphia did little to morally transform the neighborhood. In 1928 Temple's entrance requirements were tightened and the tuition raised. As one acid critic of Conwell argued, pride in Templana was transferred from moral instruction to a winning football team.[11] Hattie Wiatt and Charles Davies could never instill the pride or community feeling of a winning season. A modern university was not dependent on evangelical schemes, and a pastor intent on serving the missionary needs of environs rapidly filling with blacks might prove embarrassing. What Temple needed was a wealthy alumni which could endow for a white middle class student body housed in the suburbs, safely divorced from any moral crusade in the inner city. This was the kind of university which could safely fulfill the needs of managing a modern world.

So it was that the life of Russell Conwell reached the final chapter. The inner crisis which had shaped his career, the power of his rhetoric and the effectiveness of his style were only afterglows by the 1920's. Memorabilia and testimonials told more about the style than its health. "Acres of Diamonds," although not entirely forgotten, would be just another of many American success messages. And Temple University, although continuing to expand spectacularly was just another of many state supported urban educational complexes. Grace Church, as of this writing, still holds services at the Broad Street location, but the congregation has dwindled as dramatically as the enrollments of the university have soared. Conwell's reputation as founder is still revered among a pocket of admirers, but is no longer a charismatic institutional force. Something more than a popular man had died.

The old man seemed to sense the limited survival of his style. He wrote his daughter, Nima, on the occasion of his last contracted public lecture. He did not convey the feeling of a job well done with a hopeful eye to the future:

> *Tonight is my last professional lecture and a life work is done. It makes me feel so strange and so sad. I seem lost and useless. No more boys to help after 60 years of it. The Church has paid me to do the lecturing and I suppose will cut me down now. But I could not work on. I am too weak to walk across the room alone now.*
>
> *Your fossil old,*
>
> *Dad*[12]

Much of this pessimism can be explained as the normal lament of the physically weary aged. The feeling of futility, however, was quite consistent with the waning impact of his style. The first blow had come in the 1890's. A nervous collapse fifteen years later was not unrelated to the constrictions managerial concerns put on a flamboyant innovator. Rapidly expanding institutions had to regularize financial operations to insure their perpetuation. This task was more suited to the talents of the Bruce Bartons than the Russell Conwells. Even though Conwell was deeply concerned with urban life, *a man fully at home in the city* was functionally quite different from *one who had made his home there.*

109

The passage of the Protestant mantle from the Conwells to the Bartons had a familiar ring; it was not unlike another crucial metamorphosis in American history. Long ago, the Mathers, Cottons, and Winthrops had left their old homes to form new ones in an environment even more demanding than the American city in the late nineteenth century. The attending moral obligation was undoubtedly a greater strain on inner demands than that of Russell Conwell. The self-sacrifice needed to forge a society out of wilderness was not to be compared with the denial needed to transform rural communities into modern institutions. The Puritan founding fathers created a society; Conwell created institutions in existing society. The fact that both inherited cultures does not obviate the greater problem of social formation in seventeenth century New England. There was more continuity between nineteenth and twentieth century Americans than between the founding Puritans and their grandchildren. Cotton Mather and Soloman Stoddard were further apart than Russell Conwell and Bruce Barton.[13]

Still the stern moral codes of the Puritans and Victorians point to the transitional quality of both eras. Each transfer was complicated by the problems of individuals leaving one kind of community and trying to create another. And both were vexed with the necessity of making some kind of compromise between holding to the past and accommodating with the present. True, the half-way covenant was a more significant backsliding than the introduction of the duplex envelope for church collection, or Conwell's personalized but standardized prayer requests. Nevertheless, the demands of growth made both necessary. The needs of multiplying population and the related imperatives of system forced the compromises, adjustments and incorporations which earmark eras of massive transition. Stoddard and Barton were more comfortable in their new milieus than Mather or Conwell because the magnitude of transformation wove great strains, and great strains required wrenching inner adjustments.

Both the Puritans and the Victorians knew crises in American individualism. The first was primarily an attempt to muffle or extend individual prerogatives. The extenders were successful and spread their victory into the popular ideology of the eighteenth and early nineteenth centuries. The Victorian century saw those personal initiatives transformed into an urban-industrial institutional society. Russell Conwell trumpeted the values of individual worth at the same time he channeled them into institutional forms. He was one of countless figures who helped bring America back to a new kind of community; one which was ultimately more responsive to the demands of modern bureaucracy than the moral call of nostalgia. The irony was that the call helped seal the transformation.

The proof of the transitional character of Russell Conwell's life was its prolonged psychic crisis which was related to the stress of change at every major point: from the first abandonment of South Worthington; to the trauma of the Civil War; to the institutional endeavors in Philadelphia; and to a nervous collapse in the face of an ossifying organization. The inner disorders and resolutions were symbolic of the inner texture of American transition. Conwell's oratory and organizational talents supplied the medium of expression. His depression during the last years showed that a continuing predicament in American individualism had moved into a new setting, one requiring a different resolution. Conwell wrote a poem at the time of his second wife's death in 1910 which expressed more than a void in an old man's life:

> No one here to
> run typewriter
> to trim trees
> to drive to Northhampton
> to sit up late
> to play piano
> to help cut hay
> to go to the store
> No one to do nothing.[14]

The final paradox was upon him: The America he had run away from had now run away from him. His loneliness was writ larger than he knew.

References

[1] Bruce Barton and Russell Conwell, "Conversation Between a Young Man and an Old Man," *The American Magazine*, XCII (July, 1921), 14.

[2] Milton F. Stauffer to Millard E. Gladfelter, February 16, 1942, TC.

[3] Contemporary strains and hatred in this area are illustrated by a Community Press Release, December 18, 1969, in the Community File of TC. "From the beginning of Charette [a neighborhood plan for community renewal] Temple made no effort to recognize and accept its responsibility for human tragedy resulting from its previous history of expansion—expansion that has driven 7,000 families from this community within the last 10 years. Temple was only willing to deal with Temple's needs as defined by their 1975 expansion plans," 2.

[4] Russell H. Conwell, "Educated Criminals," *Temple Review*, XXXI, No. 15 (February 23, 1923), 2, TC. Conwell's escalating fears about the changing character of the Temple area were not unrelated to racial anxieties. See Russell H. Conwell, "Colored Migration," *Temple Review*, XXXI, No. 40 (November 30, 1923), 2-8, TC.

[5] Conwell, "Educated Criminals," 4.

[6] Robert Wiebe has expanded the meaning of vocational expertise, first delineated in *The Search for Order*, 111-132, in a new work, *The Segmented Society: An Introduction to the Meaning of America* (New York: Oxford Press, 1975). Conwell would have agreed with Wiebe's assessment of the differences between the nineteenth and twentieth centuries. In the former period Americans had "the freedom to extend local values and local enterprise as far outward as their merit allowed." In the new century, "most successful Americans reshaped their primary segments [social units] around occupational privileges . . .," 42-43.

[7] "Conversation Between a Young Man and an Old Man," 13.

[8] Warren Susman has an interesting sketch of Barton in Howard H. Quint and Milton Cantor, *Men, Women, and Issues in American History*, II (Homewood, Illinois: The Dorsey Press, 1974), 191-200.

[9] "Conversation Between a Young Man and an Old Man," 13.

[10] Russell H. Conwell to Ralph D. Sparks, August 20, 1924, TC.

[11] W. C. Crosby, "Acres of Diamonds," *American Mercury*, XIV (May, 1928), 113.

[12] Russell H. Conwell to Nima Conwell Tuttle, May 13, 1924, TC.

[13] Perry Miller shows, with consummate understanding, the huge

intellectual gulf between between the founders and their offspring in the dispute over the half-way covenant in *The New England Mind: From Colony to Province* (Boston: Beacon Press, 1953), 82-104. For a clever attack on Miller, from a social rather than intellectual perspective see Robert G. Pope, *The Half-Way Covenant: Church Membership in Puritan New England* (Princeton, New Jersey: Princeton University Press, 1969). Pope argues convincingly that the half-way covenant was a revival of religious enthusiasm and not declension. He fails to emphasize, however, Miller's major point: Something crucial to the Founder's creed was lost by relaxing the membership qualifications.

[14] Russell H. Conwell, An Untitled Poem [1010?], TC.

A NOTE ON
SOURCES AND THE DEVELOPMENT
OF AN INTERPRETATION

For a man with such wide public exposure there is surprisingly little available information on Russell Conwell. Whether or not he covered his tracks well or simply left few to follow is conjecture. Unfortunately, even for the researcher who does not plan a full biography there seems little to go on. This is particularly true for the first half of his life, or until Conwell went to Philadelphia. The only really helpful material on his mature years is in the Templana Collection of the Samuel Paley Library at Temple University in Philadelphia. There are a few other weak leads. Russell's granddaughter, Jane Conwell Tuttle of Worthington, Massachusetts, has some personal correspondence and momentos. Ms. Tuttle at this writing was ill, confined to a rest home, and has kept these sources private. Mrs. Marian Sweeny of Springfield, Massachusetts, who recently purchased part of the Conwell property at South Worthington, has a few items she found in the family barn. The most interesting is the honorable discharge Conwell received in 1870. The Worthington Historical Society has some fascinating photographs of an aging Conwell on the old homestead, but nothing substantial to remove the ignorance on Russell's early years. One old gentleman, Mr. Guy Thrasher of South Worthington, remembers his years as caretaker on the Conwell property in the early 1920's. Mr. Thrasher, however, recalls little specific about Conwell except the fact that his visits were frequent. Indeed, this writer, after visiting the South Worthington region and talking to various people who were remotely connected with

Conwell or his relatives, concluded that reliable information about Conwell's parents and his boyhood was not to be found. Sadly, conjecture became the only hope of reconstructing an interpretation of his youth.

The Templana Collection, despite its modest sources on Conwell's private life, does provide a couple of suggestive clues about the period from his Civil War days to about 1870. Particularly important is the research of the late Ms. Edith Cheney who as curator of the Templana Collection corresponded with the Department of the Army in Washington, and tried to remove the mystery surrounding Conwell's court-martial. Although never fully succeeding, she pointed to the deep significance of the Johnny Ring episode in Conwell's life. Original copies of *Conwell's Star of the North* for 1868 show that his Christian organizational endeavors in Philadelphia were outlined in his newspaper work in Minnesota. The tone of Conwell's editorials and the paper's topics also testify that the moral impact of the War did not end when the fighting stopped.

Conwell's activities in the 1870's showed a marked interest in publication. Joseph C. Carter of the Journalism Department at Temple University has edited Conwell's work as a correspondent for the *Boston Daily Evening Traveller* at the beginning of the decade. Carter's *Magnolia Journey: A Union Veteran Revisits the Former Confederate States* (1974) not only reveals a developing literary interest, but reiterates the continued impact of the War on his experience. The Templana Collection has no evidence explaining why Conwell would write several campaign biographies for Republican presidential contenders during the seventies. A single letter from Massachusetts Governor Nathaniel P. Banks to Rutherford B. Hayes in the Rutherford B. Hayes Library in Fremont, Ohio hints that Conwell had the favor of high ranking state republican politicians. Governor John Andrew had earlier acknowledged Conwell's talents as a recruiter and might have provided Banks with praise for Conwell's abilities. This, however, is speculation. Even so, loyalty to the Republican party throughout the seventies as expressed in the campaign biographies again confirms the profound imprint of the War.

The most illuminating materials of the Philadelphia years in the Templana Collection come from three quarters. First, letters from Conwell to Charles F. Stone, Melvin B. Wright, and

Arthur E. Harris who were respectively personal secretaries and an assistant minister show Conwell's growing distress after 1890. The anxieties are nearly always about finances which grew more acute as his creations expanded. Second, May Field McKean's unpublished manuscripts, "Organization and Activities of the Baptist Temple" and "The Book of Methods for the Baptist Temple," indicate that Conwell unhesitatingly favored installing modern office procedures in his home-like church, even though he resented a curtailment of his flamboyant institutional style. Third, the correspondence of Milton F. Stauffer, some of it of manuscript length, reveals that Conwell unmistakeably suffered a severe nervous collapse in 1908 or 1909. Stauffer, who remained a respected administrator at Temple University until the early 1950's, gives by far the most complete picture of the escalating personal burden Conwell carried as his institutions grew beyond his capacities.

The complete bibliography of Conwell's published works is Maurice F. Tauber's *Russell Herman Conwell, A Bibliography* (Philadelphia: Temple University, 1935). More modest bibliographies of his writings appear in three Ph.D. dissertations: Mary L. Gehring, "A Rhetorical Study of Lectures and Sermons by Russell H. Conwell," Louisiana State University, 1952; Clyde Nelson, "The Social Ideas of Russell H. Conwell," University of Pennsylvania, 1968; and Daniel W. Bjork, "Russell H. Conwell and the Crisis of American Individualism," University of Oklahoma, 1973. The Samuel Paley Library and the Templana Collection have respectively all of Conwell's published books and sermons. With the exception of "Acres of Diamonds," most of his writings have been out of print for several decades.

Since this study has emphasized the importance of rural origins, home, and related domestic matters a selected list of sermons stressing these topics is in order. It is almost impossible to find a Conwell sermon which does not allude to some aspect of "home." The following list includes only the most dramatic and explicit examples:

"Human Brotherhood," *The Temple Magazine*, V, No. 9 (March 2, 1893), 99-101.
"Liberty or Love," *The Temple Review*, XI, No. 31 (May 1, 1903), 3-6.
"Children," *The Temple Review*, XI, No. 36 (June 5, 1903), 3-5, 8.

"Marriage and Divorce," *The Temple Review*, XII, No. 33 (May 13, 1904), 3-5.

"The Country Boy in the City," *The Temple Review*, XIII, No. 16 (January 13, 1905), 3-5.

"A Boy's Visit to His Old Home," *The Temple Review*, XIII, No. 19 (February 3, 1905), 3-5.

"Large Families," *The Temple Pulpit*, XIII, No. 26 (March 24, 1905), 3-5.

"A Wedding," *The Temple Review*, XIII, No. 36 (June 2, 1905), 3-5.

"An All-Inclusive Motive," *The Temple Pulpit*, XIV, No. 5 (October 27, 1905), 3-5.

"The Best Wife," *The Temple Pulpit*, XIV, No. 8 (November 17, 1905), 3-7.

"Pilate's Wedding," *The Temple Pulpit*, XVII, No. 1 (September 25, 1908), 3-5, 8.

"The Education of Children," *The Temple Review*, XVII (March 13, 1909), 3-4.

"Seest Thou This Woman," *The Temple Pulpit*, XVII, No. 46 (August 6, 1909), 3-5.

"Telling Mother," *The Temple Pulpit*, XIX, No. 10 (December 2, 1910), 1-3.

"Whom to Marry," *The Temple Review*, XX, No. 6 (November 3, 1911), 1-3.

"Divorce," *The Temple Review*, XXI, No. 38 (July 24, 1913), 4-7.

"Dreams of Youth," *The Temple Review*, XX, No. 16 (January 12, 1912), 1-3.

"Begin at Home," *The Temple Review*, XX (November 24, 1912), 3-5, 14.

"Mother's Day," *The Temple Review*, XXI, No. 38 (July 24, 1913), 4-7.

"A Second Marriage," *The Temple Review*, XXI, No. 46 (September 18, 1913), 3-7.

"St. Valentine's Marriage Reform," *The Temple Review*, XXII, No. 20 (March 19, 1914), 3-7.

"The Mother Angel," *The Temple Review*, XXIII, No. 6 (January 28, 1915), 3-7.

"The Country Home," *The Temple Review*, XXII, No. 12 (March 23, 1916), 3-7.

"A Boy Lost," *The Temple Review*, XXIV, No. 20 (May 19, 1916), 3-6.

"Going Back Home," *The Temple Pulpit*, XXV, No. 2 (January 12, 1917), 3-5, 16.

"The Bonds of Liberty," *The Temple Review*, XXVI (January 25, 1918), 3-7.

"Home Next to Church," *The Temple Review*, XXVI, No. 11 (March 15, 1918), 3-6, 10-12.

"Lydia and Cleopatra," *The Temple Pulpit*, XXVI, No. 19 (May 10, 1918), 3-6.

"His Mother Was There," *The Temple Review*, XXVI, No. 22 (May 31, 1918), 3-6.

"An Ideal Democracy," *The Temple Review*, XXVI (November 3, 1918), 3-6.

"Our Home on Earth," *The Temple Review*, XXVII, No. 38 (November 7, 1919), 3-5.

"Our Home in Heaven," *The Temple Review*, XXVII, No. 39 (November 14, 1919), 3-7, 13.

"Mother Next to God," *The Temple Review*, XXIX, No. 5 (February 4, 1921), 1-5.

"Marriage and the Angels," *The Temple Review*, XXIX, No. 16 (April 22, 1921), 3-5.

"Honor the Dead by Helping the Living," *The Temple Review*, XXIX, No. 41 (December 2, 1921), 3-8.

"The Prodigal Son," *The Temple Review*, XXXII, No. 16 (April 18, 1924), 1-5.

The books interpreting Russell Conwell's life are without exception uncritical. The best is Agnes Rush Burr's *Russell H. Conwell and His Work*. Even though it is informative and interesting it was published in 1917 with the approval of Conwell who endorsed the book in a letter to the publisher which Burr included in the foreword. William E. Higgins' *Scaling the Eagle's Nest*, (1889) contains a few valuable clues about Conwell's boyhood, but little else. Robert Jones Burdette's *Modern Temple and the Templors* (1889) concentrates on the Temple years. Even so, Burr and Edward O. Elliott's *From Tent to Temple, a History of the Grace Baptist Church 1870 to 1895* (1946) are more helpful because the Burdette book was published before the institutional growth really unfolded. Albert Hatcher Smith's *The Life of Russell H. Conwell* also released in 1889, adds nothing which is not more skillfully presented in Higgins or Burr. The same can be said of Robert Shackleton's *Acres of Diamonds with His Life and Achievements* which is really an enlarged copy of the famous lecture, marketed in 1915 probably to sell "Acres of Diamonds" rather than a serious biography of Conwell. The only incisive critical work on Conwell was done in a debunking spirit. W. C. Crosby's essay in the *American Mercury* in 1928 is sprinkled with insights about the sources of Conwell's style. Unfortunately, in his zeal to undo a reputation Crosby missed the larger significance of his life. Slightly critical, but fully sympathetic, is Jane Conwell Tuttle's pamphlet *Life with Grandfather Conwell* which was privately printed, probably published in the early 1950's. Mrs. Tuttle gave her relative some human faults and attributed him with superhuman deeds.

Surprisingly, no one, until the present effort, has attempted to paint Conwell as a symbol of the predicament of his time. Clyde Nelson's dissertation nicely covers his social ideas while avoiding the larger problem of their relationship to transitional change—particularly that of a psychological nature. Mary L. Gehring was interested in Conwell as an elocutionist. Since her dissertation was written for a speech department this was only fitting. The present writer made a preliminary effort in his dissertation to synthesize Conwell's ideas with his time in order to illuminate the social quality of American transition. Yet he was not perceived simply and totally as a symbol. The result was little insight into the representative possibilities of his inner crisis.

As the primary sources were meager and yet Conwell seemed to mirror a broader dilemma deep in the American condition, suggestive work in American intellectual history helped focus the man in the era. At the same time, these studies sent the writer into other disciplines—particularly psychology—which led to a plausible explanation of Conwell's experience. Two superb interpretations of American transition since the mid-nineteenth century opened the way. First, George M. Fredrickson's *The Inner Civil War: Northern Intellectuals and the Crisis of the Union* (1965) turned attention to the impact of the War on the attitudes of New Englanders toward society and themselves. And, Robert Wiebe's *The Search for Order, 1877-1920 (1967)* emphasized the strain which resulted when an agrarian inward-looking society faced the coming of modernity. These works opened the door, but did not concentrate on the significance of one individual as a window into the larger issue of national transition.

William G. McLoughlin did just that in *The Meaning of Henry Ward Beecher: An Essay on the Shifting Values of Mid-Victorian America, 1840-1870* (1970). Here was an attempt to show a popular man as representative of the way nineteenth century Americans coped with the materialism and uncertainties of transition. But McLoughlin's essay did more; it pointed to the important problem of Victorian belief in the coming of modernity. Walter E. Houghton's older *The Victorian Frame of Mind 1830-1870* (1957) was a convincing piece of writing which suggested McLoughlin was skirting a deeper problem than his study of Beecher revealed. Houghton's analysis showed the Victorians were fundamentally unhappy in an era of transition and pointed toward a profound psychological struggle.

At this stage of rethinking, the significance of Russell Conwell as a symbol began to take a new shape, one which moved into the much maligned and yet fascinating subdiscipline Eric Erikson called psychohistory. Three compelling interpretations of three widely disparate lives generated a different more challenging look at Conwell's experiences, which then appeared in much sharper perspective—a stance adding to his representative character. Erikson's *Young Man Luther: A Study in Psychoanalysis and History* (1958) was a revelation on the significance of a youthful identity crisis and inner struggle. Arthur Mitzman's *The Iron Cage: An Historical Interpretation of Max Weber* (1969) showed with brilliance how a sociologist could use psychology to illuminate the significance of a major thinker's writing and personal life. And, Ann Jardin's *The First Henry Ford: A Study in Personality and Business Leadership* (1971) turned the writer's thoughts to the major place of abandonment and return in American life.

One more work was of crucial importance in securing an interpretive frame to order the smattering of evidence available on Conwell's life. Gene Wise has recently called the attention of American historians to the importance of symbol in the written record. *American Historical Explanations: A Strategy for Grounded Inquiry* (1973) reiterated an often forgotten essential in the historian's method. Interpretation is his most significant obligation, not something he attaches to research as an afterthought. Such a faith helped find a way to define the significance of Russell Conwell.

INDEX

74n; reaction to Jenny Hayden's death, 16, 21; Johnny Ring legend, 1, 10-12, 25, 38n, 39n; last lecture, 109; law practice, 15-16; law school, 13-14; at Lexington Baptist Church, 16-17; his marriages, 13, 16; move into the ministry, 17; Minnesota years 14-16, 22, 25, 40n; his modern style, 79-91, 94-99; move to Philadelphia, 18-19; his nervous breakdown, 33, 47n, 71, 109; as newspaper correspondent, 9, 15, 38n; his oratory, 5, 7-8, 15, 11; his ordination, 17; his interpretation of "overreaching" institutions, 65-67; his parents, 1, 2, 5, 6, 7, 14, 16, 21, 54; on prayer, 110; poem of, 111; presidential campaign biographies, 15, 41n, 42n; his psychic difficulties, 11-12, 21, 22, 25, 28, 29, 31-33, 58, 64-65, 90-91, 93, 99, 109, 110, 111; on public morality, 80-84, 108; as recruiter for the union army, 7, 9, 22, 25; role changing—effect of, 14-15, 22-23, 94, 107-108; experience as a runaway, 4-5, 34; his shoulder wound, 9, 15, 38n, 40n; Temple College—founding of, 24-27, 45n, 46n; Temple University Medical Center—founding of, 29-30, 46n, 47n; testimonials on, 91-94, 109; at Tremont Temple, 15, 37n; on urban crime, 106; will of, 35; on women, marriage, and divorce, 56-65, 83-84; at Yale College, 6, 37n

Conwell, Sarah Sanborn (second wife), 16, 19, death of 33, 55, 56, 61

Cottons (family), 110

Darwinian science, 22
Davies, Charles M., role in the founding of Temple College, 24-25; 29, 108
Deacons, 18, 29, 91-92, 94, 107
Depression, the 1870s, 18; the 1890s, 30, 66
Dewey, John, 83
Divorce, 57-58; (see Conwell on women, divorce, and marriage)
Don Juan, 56
Douglass, Frederick, 2
Drexel, Anthony, 26
Drexel Institute, 26
Duplex envelope, 88, 110

Eagle's Nest, 37n, 92
ego, 97-99

125